FAMI
Sabbath
TRADITIONS

TO BLESS YOUR HEART AND HOME

Filling the Sabbath hours with joy

Millie & John Youngberg

ADVENTIST FAMILY TRADITIONS

Pacific Press® Publishing Association
Nampa, Idaho
Oshawa, Ontario, Canada

Edited by Jerry D. Thomas
Designed by Michelle C. Petz
Cover photo: Caucasian family © copyright Eyewire, Inc.
African-American family © copyright Photodisc, Inc.
Interior photos: pp. 9, 47, 69, 78, 108, 120, 126, 133 c/o Millie and John Youngberg
pp. 73, 95, 100 © copyright Eyewire, Inc.
pp. 19, 30, 57, 130 © copyright Photodisc, Inc.
Interior line art: pp. 97, 98 by Michelle C. Petz

Printed in the United States of America

ISBN: 0-8163-1854-9 African-American cover
0-8163-1848-4 Caucasian cover

Contents

Preface

The Sabbath is a gift from God, given not only to Adam and Eve, but to all generations. It is a time of communion with God and family and fellowship with the family. It is the family day.

We are aware that the Sabbath is very important to God. He would like us to enjoy the sacred hours of the Sabbath as a delight with our families. It seems that the family and the Sabbath just go together and they should, because that was part of God's plan at the time of Creation.

In our worldwide travels we have been made aware that there is a great need for teaching Seventh-day Adventist families how to keep the Sabbath day holy and with joy. We all have much to learn. For some families the Sabbath may be just a "holiday" and not necessarily a "holy day." For others it is a "don't-do-this-or-that" day. Our own Sabbaths have ranged from a ho-hum experience to a dynamic powerful day when we have felt very near to God. It is our desire that by sharing our experience it may help others to enjoy the Sabbath in a more positive way.

I (Millie) have come a long way from not keeping the Sabbath at all. I was a teenager working as a cashier in a theater on Friday evening and staying home on the Sabbath Day to rest. I used to feel bored, so I would clean the dresser drawers. With age and maturity I began to experience more and more appropriate ways of keeping God's special day. But though I have come a long way I feel there still is room for improvement.

And maybe that is where you are too . . . searching.

Our Prayer

Praise be to You, O God our Father, for showing us daily Your wonderful love, and for giving us the Sabbath as a gift of time, to remember our Creator.

We praise You for calling us to "come apart and rest awhile," and inviting us into the shelter of Your presence, hiding us from the intrigues of men.

This is the day that You have made, the Sabbath of the Lord our God. This day You set the lonely in families, and lead forth the prisoner with singing, the day You refresh Your weary inheritance and answer us with awesome deeds of righteousness as we heed your words of blessing and comfort, "Thou shalt rest."

How priceless is Your unfailing love! (Psalm 36:7).

We welcome Your holy presence, our Creator, Redeemer and Friend, the Hope of all the ends of the earth and of the farthest seas.

You are the praise of Your people, for on this holy day You let us feast on the abundance of Your house and give us drink from the river of delight. For with You is the fountain of life, in Your light, we see light (Psalm 36:8, 9).

From the rising of the sun, to the place where it sets, Your Name, O Lord, is to be praised (Psalm 113:3).

How to Use this Book

1. Read for personal interest or for ways of sparking up your own family's Sabbath time.

2. The materials in this book may be used by families to enhance their Sabbath celebration experience. Ideas are given for Sabbath activities. There are Sabbath songs to sing and Jewish celebration activities to enjoy. *Family Sabbath Traditions* contains a collection of materials that can be used by any family. If the ages in the family are appropriate, read it together and participate in the activities given. Perhaps using *Family Sabbath Traditions* on Friday evening at worship time would be a blessing to the family.

3. Have a weekend Family Sabbath Celebration Seminar with the local church, the district or just those interested. The group can be a small group or a large one. Different individuals may be assigned certain chapters for the instruction and others might lead out in strategies given. All this may be accomplished without much preparation time.

4. Start a fellowship group of several families who are interested in enhancing their families' Sabbath experience. Meet once a week to discuss a chapter or two. Make it easy on the leader by asking each person to

bring his or her copy of this book. Each person reads a paragraph or section and discusses with the group. The one person reading might ask the group a question that will lead to further discussion. Close by praying for the children and personal needs of those participating. To expand the experience have the parents volunteer a demonstration of a creative family worship for the Sabbath on certain assigned dates. Later draw the children into the planning session and have them prepare a Sabbath evening's worship. They can be extremely creative!

5. Buy the book and give it to each newly baptized member of your church. Agree on a time to go through the book with each new member. Or even better, spend Friday evenings or Sabbath afternoons with a new member, reading the chapters of the book and experiencing a Sabbath day of rest together. This can be a beautiful ministry.

CHAPTER ONE

"The Sabbath should be made so interesting to our families that its weekly return will be hailed with joy . . . thus parents can make the Sabbath...the most joyful day of the week. They can lead their children to regard it as a delight" (CHILD GUIDANCE, P. 537).

A JOYFUL EXPERIENCE

EXTRAVAGANZA CELEBRATION

As the new millennium's zero hour neared, millions gathered in joyful extravaganzas, waiting for the clocks to roll over from 999 to 000. On our television screens, we saw where the millennium would begin at the International Dateline. First we saw fireworks at Caroline Island, the most easterly of the Karibati Islands in the South Pacific where the day begins. Then we saw the landing of a flotilla of canoes right at the beach auditorium in New Zealand as heart-gripping folk music was sung by some of the world's finest opera stars.

In Sydney, Australia the famous bridge had a glittering sign that read "Eternity!" and the millions joined in what they considered to be a "world party." Viewers of television were transported to Beijing where they saw dignitaries in their gala attire and the colorful and graceful Chinese singers and dancers. Soon we saw the excitement at the Eiffel Tower in Paris with dazzling fireworks, and then we caught sight of an exotic cruise ship on a lake high in the Argentinian Andes with skilled musicians playing folklore songs. Everyone was excited!

What were we celebrating? The world was living the kind of moment that would not be repeated for another thousand years! All peoples united in celebrating what most believed to be the grandest, most spectacular event of their lifetimes.

What throbbing anticipation in people groups everywhere as they prepared for the extravaganza, which crescendoed as the climactic hour was being ushered in time zone by time zone around the planet!

Since it was Friday evening, our family's preparation was to welcome in not only the new millennium, but also the Sabbath! We assembled in church before the sundown hour, the hour we knew the new millennium year really would begin.

Quite unlike the noisy celebration at Times Square where the lighted ball came sliding down to announce the year 2000, we celebrated with singing, sharing, eating, and an inspirational message from Pastor Dwight Nelson. We celebrated not with cocktails and rock music, but with the Holy Spirit's rejoicing power as we prayed in the new millennium. We feasted on an aromatic potluck supper and then feasted in prayer. The midnight toll of the bell found all on our knees pleading for readiness for Christ's soon return. And, praise God, when celebrating His way, there were no hangovers the next day–just exhilarating memories!

This new millennium extravaganza was truly spectacular all throughout the world, but it was nothing in comparison to the Second Coming celebration all throughout the universe for us who love Jesus and keep His commandments!

I (Millie) used to think that a celebration called for throwing a big party. But seasoned experience has taught me that I can have a joyful celebration time with my church family, or with John at some lovely spot in our own home by the fireplace or in the summer breeze amongst the fragrant flowers in the back yard as the sun in the west goes down on yet another busy week.

Many Adventists don't feel that the Sabbath is a time for a real celebration, but is just a quiet evening at home reading the *Review* and the Bible, or visiting. The purpose of this book is to stimulate awareness of the Sabbath as so special that we anticipate it as a spiritual celebration. A special day. A holy day.

I am wondering how we can really celebrate the Sabbath—or is "celebrate" the "Adventist-appropriate" word? But as one contemplates the marvels of Creation and the closure of that dynamic week by the Creator God—there just has to be some kind of celebration!

When I conclude one of my busy weeks, replete with activities and accomplishments, I am ready to ooooh and aaaah as I recall how God "recreated" my strength all week to meet those challenges. I am ready to celebrate the Sabbath and to welcome some rest. I am ready to be recharged, and to be pampered just a bit. I am ready to take more time communicating with God the Father.

Do you feel the same way?

Thank You, Father, for the Sabbath

It is Satan himself who tries to intimidate us earthling Christians by telling us that we can in no way keep the Sabbath Day holy. Satan does everything in his power to occupy the believers' time and prevent us from worshiping the Father on His Sabbath Day of rest. Satan wants us to show disrespect for the fourth commandment. And he wants us to give up.

But thanks be to God, for He gives us the victory! The Sabbath has become a special day of the week for us who love Jesus and desire to keep His perfect law. To us, Sabbath is indeed a joyful celebration day! God's perfect law is perfect love.

God, in Your wisdom and love, You provide us a day off from our weekly duties of work and school, and bless us with a day to worship You in love and thanksgiving. Thank You, Father, for this beautiful gift of time, free to us all—rich and poor alike.

Celebrating With Jesus, Our Heavenly Guest

Jesus has been present in our home all week. Still, on Preparation Day, we energetically concentrate on making our home as clean and tidy as if we anticipate a distinguished, new Guest. This flurry toward readiness somehow signals us—as the host family—and our resident Guest that we are readying to receive Him from "in our home" into a closer, more-intimate-than-ever, uninterrupted 24-hour reception "in our hearts."

The moment comes. Relaxed around the fireplace, we sing our traditional "Day Is Dying in the West," followed by Sabbath Eve worship. Now the lights are dimmed. Family-style, we gradually sprawl out over the floor and sofa. Curly Dog interrupts our pensive thoughts as she jumps over us from one to another for her back scratching and a playful pat.

We are quiet in our own deep thoughts: *How nice if the doorbell would ring just now, and, when we open it, Jesus is here with His joyful smile to say, "I've come to your house tonight to be with you during the Sabbath hours. You see, I also like to come apart to rest on this special day, and tonight I would be greatly pleased to join you. Will you let Me in?"*

Family Activity

Dialogue:

- How would you greet Jesus? What would you tell Him? What would you ask Him?
- He would have something to tell you. What might it be?
- Do you think this would be a joyful experience? Would you tell anyone about your Visitor?
- How do you imagine your visit with your heavenly Guest?

Preparing for Your Heavenly Guest

As we plan for the Sabbath, we are preparing for our heavenly Guest, are we not? Often we are not aware that a heavenly Guest is in our home. Some families even leave an empty plate for their special Guest as a reminder of His presence.

I am reminded of the occasion after the crucifixion of Jesus as He was walking along the road to Emmaus when two weary travelers with compassion invited Him to their home for the evening. Not until the holy Guest had blessed the meal were they aware that the invited One was Jesus. Their hearts thrilled within them, and then Jesus was gone.

True, Jesus is not "gone" from our homes after the Sabbath, but is the Sabbath sometimes already "gone" before we realize that we missed the special blessing of our special Guest on His special day? Are we sometimes left to regret that we have to "grind out" another whole work week before the special day off with Jesus comes again?

Next Sabbath when your family and your home

are in readiness, visualize yourself bowing and worshiping King Jesus. Every week all over the world for 24 hours, multitudes on earth and all of heaven are doing just that! The Sabbath is kept at the appointed time in the different time zones when the King of kings and Lord of lords is worshiped—in the little jungle village or up in high-rises in the big cities, along with Elijah, Moses, and Enoch in heaven. We Sabbath keepers are all connected in some process of keeping the day holy as we were commanded at Creation.

Through the Holy Spirit, Jesus is present in each home from which worship ascends. Songs and prayers and "thank-You's" are expressed in all languages. God, the Linguist, understands them all; they are to Him as the sound of lapping of many waters—a joyful noise unto the Lord—as David expresses it in the Psalms.

When Jesus is present, it is something to celebrate! For example, if Queen Elizabeth were to come to my home, would I celebrate? I know so. How about the president of our country? Much more to be exalted, we have the President of the Universe in our homes and we are celebrating Creation with Him. Awesome thought!

Are we preparing our hearts and homes with joyful anticipation for the President of the Universe to enter? Are we celebrating His presence with us?

Then how do we do it?

Celebrating the Birthday of the World

God worked for six days to create a whole new world. Then He rested for one day to fully enjoy the work and pleasure of His hands. He enjoyed it so much that He wanted to bestow us with the same pleasure. This seventh day is set aside for our privilege of also putting aside everything that is secular, and spending time in communicating with God and one another. Sabbath is a day of joy and rest—a gift of God—given not only to Adam and Eve, but to all. It is the family day. God wants us to be happy and to spend quality time with our family on the Sabbath.

Most families look forward eagerly to at least a one-week vacation every year. Why would we want to give up our God-promised one day vacation every week? God didn't just offer us this day off. And He did more than promise it. God commanded this day off. It is thus a day off that is perfectly guilt-free!

In Bible time Jews called the Sabbath "the Queen," a royal name because it was so superlatively special to them.

Parents Model Sabbath Celebration

My friend once inquired of her neighbor whether she attended the 8:20 "early service" or "regular service" at 11:20 A.M. "Oh, no, not early church," the neighbor responded. "We'd be back home so early that dinner would be over by noon, and that would make too long an afternoon for Lisa. Otherwise, by the time we eat and clear dinner after regular service, there's only a couple of hours to fill before vespers," said the mother. "I don't want her whining by the middle of the afternoon, "How much longer until we can go to the mall?"

In happy contrast, a Christian mother from the Caribbean Islands reflects on memories of delightful Sabbaths when she was a child:

"They are good memories," she begins. "My parents left their offspring a good example of Sabbath observance and celebration. Three months after my father was baptized he married my mother, who had been a Sabbath keeper all her life. Since there were seven children, it was quite a job to get us all ready for Sabbath, but Mother and Father did it. My father took Sabbath observance seriously and my mother was a good role model for Father and us.

"Mother would remind us of the Sabbath throughout the whole week, and on Friday from the time we got up. Sabbath preparation was important to her. Laundry was done on Sunday so our Sabbath dresses were always ready a week ahead. On Thursday Father would cut the grass and tidy the yard. On Friday Mother would get up early to clean the house and prepare delicious meals for Sabbath Eve and Sabbath.

"When we children came home from school, we had to first clean our rooms, polish our shoes, and then help Mother finish cleaning the house. Everyone was rushing to get ready before sundown. After our baths, we girls put on clean dresses for the opening of Sabbath.

"Everything was clean inside and outside our house. Inside the tempting aromas from the kitchen filled the home. Mom wanted the family to be ready at least 30 minutes before sundown. As the sun set, we were seated in the living room singing our favorite religious songs, waiting to welcome the Sabbath.

"Sabbath was a special day, when we would thank and praise God for His blessings of the week, and a time we enjoyed each other.

"During those family worships on Friday evenings, we sang our favorite songs, recited together Psalm 91 or the fourth commandment. Some shared their favorite Bible story or verse. Often my Dad read a thought from a favorite devotional writer. Frequently he would check whether we knew our memory verse and Bible story for the week. The family formed our prayer circle, and one or two would pray. Worship was concluded by singing 'Welcome, Blessed Sabbath Day.' Last, all nine of us would hug and wish each other 'Happy Sabbath!'

"Mom always had some sweet treat to make Friday night supper different for us. After worship, we frequently went to bed early since there were so many of us to get ready for church in the morning. We were up soon after sunrise, Mom first. She already had all the dresses, shoes, socks, and bows ready for us.

"With shiny faces, pretty dresses and bows, and the best boys' clothes, off to church we would go—all nine of us. Since church was only a short distance, we all walked—together. That was the way Dad wanted it.

"Although we were poor, Sabbath dinner was something different from other meals, and was delicious. Sometimes we would stay home in the afternoon and play Bible games, or listen to more Bible stories from our parents. Often we would go on a nature walk or go to a nearby cave, or waterfall. Other times there were church activities for us."

My Caribbean friend concluded, "Although both Dad and Mom are gone now, and I am an adult myself, I still remember the way they kept the Sabbath. As a mother now, I try to do my best in following their footsteps. We plan so that the Sabbath is as enjoyable as possible for the children."

Some readers may think that this is a little beyond what we can manage for our children nowadays. If so, what options could your family adopt at this time that would make Sabbath an outstanding day—a delightful day?

Parents, you have the privilege of teaching good principles of Sabbath keeping to your children in order that they might not depart from the Word of God. In turn, your children may transmit to another generation the joys and benefits of the Sabbath. Please take advantage of the little time you have to teach your children about Jesus, and the true, and the good, and the beautiful. Lead them toward eternal life!

So, let's make the Sabbath special to our families: appealing, enjoyable, pleasant, exceptional, unique, exclusive, extraordinary—and yet holy, for it is not a common day. The Sabbath is God's day—and in keeping it holy we are celebrating the birthday of His world!

Chapter Two

"I also gave the My Sabbath, to be a sign between them and Me, that they might know that I am the Lord who sanctifies them."

(Ezekiel 20:12)

Sabbath Is God's Idea

Whose idea is the Sabbath anyhow? Was it Moses' idea? Is it the idea of some people who just want to be out-of-step with the rest of the world as we enter the third millennium of the Christian era? So whose idea was it?

There were gorgeous flowers carpeting the earth with living green. Sun, moon, stars, in the sky overhead, bright-plumaged birds caroling their songs in the air, and the sea teeming with fish. The forest and plain were full of joyful tame animals. Then God set aside a time when He could communicate with man and woman which He called the Sabbath.

The couple had time for Him and He would have fellowship time with them. He instructed them to remember the Sabbath and meted out the time parameters of their existence—six days of happy, joyful work, then one day of rest. As that first Friday in Eden drew toward its close, God decreed the institution of marriage creating the bond between man and woman, and then He decreed the institution of the Sabbath creating for the couple time for their mutual fellowship and time for their fellowship with Him. This was for the happiness of Adam and Eve and it would be for the happiness of the future generations that would populate the earth.

The Sabbath was unique in that God Himself had rested, blessed, and hallowed it. It was the perpetual reminder to them that He is the Creator, the great Benefactor.

God thought it was a good plan and He was pleased with what He saw: "Behold, it was very good." It is very good that we have the Sabbath.

The Sabbath was God's idea and He invested in it a beauty beyond the wildest imagination as part of a creative package for man. For the Sabbath was made for man (humankind) (Mark 2:27).

Family Activity

Why was God's plan for the Sabbath "very good"?

A Reminder of the Creator

Satan attacked the Sabbath that God said was very good. He didn't want allegiance to be given to the real Creator. He said it didn't matter what day is kept holy and has attempted to keep the world's inhabitants from worshiping the true Creator.

But God says, "observe the Sabbath." It is impossible to keep the Sabbath and forget it's Creator—Jesus. The Sabbath is a reminder of the Creator whose we are.

So as we keep the Sabbath in its 24-hour period, we . . .

- Worship God
- Remember who created us
- Have fellowship time
- Have time for prayer and Bible study

Our friend, Esther Knott, tells of meeting Alias Alaby one day at the university cafeteria. He was new in the faith and she sensed that there must be a story behind the headline. "Tell me about your first Sabbath," she suggested. Tears filled his eyes at the memory, and he began to share a precious chapter of his walk with the Lord. He had been a minister of an evangelical denomination for many years and was editing and marketing books on the Bible as poetry. The heaviest day of selling books was Sunday as he rushed from church to church. Burdened and too busy, he never found time to rest. His wife Edith suggested that they both needed to take a day off. Alias answered, "Yes, but which day?"

At that moment they were driving past a Seventh-day Adventist church, and glancing in that direction Edith said, "You should take Saturday off." As a child she had attended an Adventist elementary school for four years and had fond memories of the experience. The next Friday at work, Alias decided he would keep the Sabbath. He traveled home quickly hoping to get there before sunset. The road took him through the mountains and as the sun neared the horizon God brushed the canvas of the heavens with one of the most spectacular sunsets he had ever seen. It was as if God was going out of His way to rejoice that someone else out there had accepted His invitation to fellowship.

When Professor Alaby got home he greeted the family with, "Happy Sabbath!" It was all so new to them, that they weren't exactly sure what was happening. The whole family joined in welcoming the Sabbath for the first time.

The next day, the Alabys went to Sabbath School and the worship service. It was their first Sabbath, February 25, 1995. Four years later he was baptized. But it was hard for him to express all of his feelings about that first Sabbath. He had a feeling of gratitude. He knew that the God of the universe had invited him to rest and fellowship. Alias says: "I need the Sabbath, and that is why God gave it to me. Praise His name!"

God, Who made us, knew at Creation what our human machinery needs. So He made a rule—no work for 24 hours each week. He created in us a body rhythm that requires a one-day vacation in every seven for the sake of body and spirit. Our overstressed lives need time out to recharge our batteries. And even our children don't have to do homework that day. They too need a day off.

Birthday Celebration

Birthdays motivate joyous celebrations. Why? My birthday is a celebration of my very existence, a time to affirm my personal identity. My birthday reminds me of who I am and whose I am.

God could have memorialized Creation with a magnificent monument of marble, many miles high. But it would be seen only by those geographically close. He chose instead to build a monument of time, for a span of time is available to us all.

In choosing the frequency of time for a memorial, God might have chosen a yearly event. But in His wisdom, He knew that we need a more frequent, weekly memorial. And so He chose to help us remember every seven days who made the world and to whom we belong. We know, do we not, how people who honor only two memorials a year, Christmas and Easter, tend to forget worship the time in-between?

Wedding Celebration

Do you like to go to weddings? Typically weddings are occasions of great joy. What joy there must have been as Creation week advanced to a close! It was then, on the sixth day, that the first wedding between a man and a woman was celebrated.

Then, a few hours later as the sun was setting, God celebrated another wedding—a wedding between humankind and God! The onset of sundown signaled the Sabbath—that special time for the Creator and His beloved to be alone. Indeed, God set aside every weekly Sabbath for this ongoing love relationship.

Without this love, however, the Sabbath will become a mere drag. Just as one cannot fake joy in other relationships, one cannot fake joy in the Sabbath relationship with the Creator. But if we love the Lord of the Sabbath, the Sabbath will be the happiest day of the week!

Perhaps this thoughtful self-examination is in order: *Am I more worried about breaking the Sabbath than I am about breaking my relationship with the Lord of the Sabbath?*

The Fourth Commandment

To protect His weekly "wedding anniversary" with us, God set the love in a "commandment." It is His fourth command, and the only one to begin with the word "Remember." (Did God know the human tendency to forget anniversaries?)

Since the Sabbath anniversary reminder is so important to God, it may be well to understand it thoroughly and even to memorize it. I (Millie) had been a Seventh-day Adventist for some time before I memorized this important commandment, which I felt the Lord was encouraging me to do.

I find, however, that unless I frequently repeat this fourth commandment, found in Exodus 20:8-11, I tend to forget it. The law of the mind is still true: If you don't use it, you lose it. Friday sunset worship is an excellent time to repeat this important commandment—alone, or as a couple, or with the whole family. (You will enjoy the activity at the end of the chapter.)

Some of the key words are *rested, blessed,* and *hallowed* (Genesis 2 uses rested, blessed, and sanctified).

Cause and Effect

A law of life is that when we put something into an effort, we are more likely to get something out. There is in-flow and out-flow. What comes out depends on what goes in.

God "put in" the Sabbath three components: *rest, blessing, and hallowing/sanctification* (Genesis 2:1-3).

What can we "get out" of the Sabbath? *Rest, blessing, and sanctification.*

I can receive rest on the Sabbath. In a passage of Scriptures whose context is the Sabbath, Jesus said: "Come to me, all you who are weary and burdened, and I will give you rest" (Matthew 11:28). I can receive *blessing* from the Sabbath. Isaiah 58:14 says that Sabbath keepers will delight themselves in the Lord and ride on the high places of the earth. And more than this, God even promises to "sanctify" more than the Sabbath—He will sanctify us also! "I also gave them My Sabbath, to be a sign between them and Me, that they might know that I am the Lord who sanctifies them" (Ezekiel 20:12).

If we are to be sanctified, it follows that it is pretty

important to know what the word means! The definition is "to set apart for a holy use." In other words, when we honor Him in close communion on the Sabbath, He is able to make known His distinctive plan for our lives—ultimately our greatest happiness.

The Sabbath and Family Belong Together

Some years ago we invited a well-known husband and wife team as guest presenters at Family Life International. The couple hosts one of the most popular daily religious broadcasts in the evangelical world. At noon we honored them with a special meal. As we dined together, this gracious gentleman queried about the beliefs of Seventh-day Adventists. I responded that the family and the Sabbath both had been bequeathed to us at Creation and we believe that they belong together.

A faraway look came into the gentleman's eyes and I almost could see the "wheels turning in his head." Later his wife published a book on how to make Sunday special for the family. Although the couple did not understand our seventh-day Sabbath, they did have it right that the day of worship and the family belong together.

The institutions of the Sabbath and the family have more in common, however, than their mutual bestowal to humankind in the Garden of Eden: they both have been the subject of particular, peculiar attack by "the enemy." But—praise God—He has not allowed either attack to be universal or eternal.

Satan's attack on the Sabbath proposed to set in place a breach in the first table of the law to break our covenant love relationship with our Creator God.

Satan's forceful attack on the family proposed to set in place a breach in the second table of the law to break our covenant love relationship with our families. With viciousness Satan has attacked marriage fidelity to break relationships between spouses. Also, in Western culture today Satan has made a concerted effort to "free" children from obedience to their parents, creating a rebellious atmosphere that has much of the world ripe for anarchy.

"Back to Eden" in the Sabbath plan and "Back to Eden" in the Marriage/Family plan is still God's plan for "Eden Restored."

God's Double Blessing

The Family and the Sabbath belong together. They are God's double blessing.

1. The Creation account in Genesis records two weddings:
   - day six was the wedding between man and woman
   - day seven was the wedding between God and humankind.
2. The Ten Commandments reinforce the two Eden institutions
   - the seventh day as the birthday of the world (fourth commandment)
   - marriage as the celebration of love (seventh commandment)
3. The fourth commandment says—
   "Remember your ROOTS" (Creation)
4. The fifth commandment says–
   "Honor your ROOTS" (family)
5. Holy means restored or set apart for relationship.

- The Sabbath is holy (Exodus 20:8).
- Marriage is holy (Malachi 2:11).

6. In the last days there will be a "restoration of all things" (Acts 3:21). The two Eden institutions that were begun together, under the last day message, will be restored together:
   - The Sabbath will be restored (Isaiah 58:12-14).
   - The family will be restored (Malachi 4:5, 6) for the Elijah Message will turn the hearts of the parents to their children, and the hearts of the children to their parents. Christ said that Elijah, when he comes, "will restore all things" (Matthew 17:11).

God's Antidote for Burnout

In this fast-moving age where drivers talk on the cell phone with one hand, eat a burger with the other, and steer with their knees—where the fingers click on a computer mouse connecting them with shifting sensory overload on the World Wide Web—where laborers work the midnight shift going through endless motions with little meaning—the burnout casualties are increasing. The body needs rest for at least 24 hours. Psychologists indicate that incomplete action cycles are an important factor in cases of burnout. What this means is that we start things that we don't finish. The backlog comes deeper and deeper as we "layer on" more unfinished projects. God, in His love and wisdom, provides a way to break these cycles.

The Sabbath is designed to bring a sense of completeness to our incomplete work in life. We are to cease "as if our work were done," reminding ourselves that only God can make our work and lives complete.

Christ proclaimed, "It is finished!" on the cross and rested on the Sabbath. We are to view our work in weekly segments in the light of His accomplishment!

In God's answer to human frenzy and stress, He points our unmet needs back to Eden. In the Sabbath rest we can fulfill our need of peace. Both in the marriage institution and within the church family we can find fulfillment to our human need for companionship.

Family Activity

How can we easily memorize the fourth commandment? Here is one method. Notice each phrase in the left column. Memorize one phrase at a time. In the right column, to jog your memory until you have dominated the sequence, is the first letter of each word. The first word is provided to ensure everyone a good start.

Example:

Remember the Sabbath day	Remember t S d
to keep it holy.	t k i h
Six days you shall labor	S d y s l
and do all your work,	a d a y w
but the seventh day is the Sabbath	b t s d i t S
of the Lord your God.	o t L y G
In it you shall do no work:	I i y s d n w
you,	y
nor your son,	n y s
nor your daughter,	n y d
nor your male servant,	n y m s
nor your female servant,	n y f s
nor your cattle,	n y c

nor your stranger who is within your gates.	n y s w i w y g
For in six days the Lord made the heavens	F i s d t L m t h
and the earth,	a t e
the sea,	t s
and all that is in them,	a a t i i t
and rested the seventh day.	a r t s d
Therefore the Lord blessed the Sabbath	T t L b t S
and hallowed it.	a h i.

When you have memorized the verse, move on by removing the prompters.

Family Activity

After the fourth commandment has been memorized, as a family or small group discuss what each phrase of the commandment is saying to you and the family.

Chapter Three

"While preparation for the Sabbath is to be made all through the week, Friday is to be the special preparation day"

(Testimonies, Volume 1:354).

Planning for the Sabbath

The Most Joyful Day

Is joy something we can wish for—and there it is? That's all there is to it? If we can think of it, we can have it? We have discovered that Sabbath joy doesn't just happen on its own. Mingled prayer and planning are imperative to make Sabbath the most joyful day of the week. How can we ask God to bless what we haven't even thought of, much less endeavored to act upon?

The Time-challenged

Let's not pretend that planning is easy: When Mom works outside of the home and/or has small children, there are huge obstacles to getting everything done at home. And in our modern society, there are millions who commute from the suburbs to downtown who spend many hours crawling along freeways in traffic jams. Some employees don't get off work until 4:00 or 5:00 on Friday afternoons. Then there are those priceless souls who have gone the second mile in "wonderful service" for the church all week in addition to their livelihoods.

No matter how hard one tries, there are times that the "cut off" point comes and the work is not finished. God knew that—left to ourselves as our work continues—we would never find that point. So He made it perfectly clear when we should cut it off: Sundown. Stop.

When our work is not done, there is only one way to stop. Stop. Esther Knott recalls how she was rushing to finish some laundry before the Sabbath when she realized that it could not be finished in time. She said to herself, "What is folded is folded. What is done is done, and what is not done is not done." Sometimes the only solution is to "pull the plug!"

Now picture the coming Sabbath as "the Queen" coming to visit your home. What would you do to prepare for royalty? Your list might include attention to shoes, garments, baths, hair, cooking, tidying, cleaning, and—especially "making things right."

Planning for Preparation Day

Let's intensify the commandment a bit: "Remember the Sabbath day [all week, for I will want] to keep it holy [when it comes]."

Simply put, Preparation Day doesn't begin on Friday; Preparation Week ends on Friday. On Sabbath afternoon we are already headed into the next week's Sabbath School lesson in the quarterly. On

Sunday, as Paul suggests, we are to lay aside our next Sabbath's offering. So by Monday shouldn't we be rolling right along?

During Sunday morning worship it is also timely to update the family of the upcoming Friday sunset time, and the time in mind for Friday evening worship. These times can then be prominently posted among the refrigerator art. The family can also decide who will lead out in the two special worships on Friday and Sabbath evenings, and whether there is a special location for Sabbath afternoon activities coming to mind. It is also a good time to ask if anyone already has any input on church-planned or other desired or "do good" activities that day. One mother told her sons that they could give some suggestions for Sabbath activities and that if they didn't come up with any ideas, their parents would have some.

Another mentionable at this time is who next Sabbath's guests, if any, might be. If expense is a factor, you might consider hosting a potluck meal with another family or two with same-age children and invite each family to also be responsible for one Sabbath afternoon activity. Remember the single-parent families, the lonely students, the seniors, and the discouraged: "Christ keeps an account of every expense incurred in entertaining for His sake. He supplies all that is necessary for this work" (*Testimonies,* V1:344, emphasis supplied).

When Friday does come—and it will—it can be a disaster day in many homes if one person is left with all the unfinished work. A division of labor is needed throughout the family. Especially should each person be responsible for putting his/her room in order. A family council may be in order here, giving children a choice of the preparation jobs, and whether they will rotate them by week. Some families choose to draw job slips from a bowl. Others place the "job cards" on the corresponding bedroom doors. Some find personalized cards at the kitchen table with a note of appreciation for the last preparation day jobs, along with the new schedule. Some families simply use the volunteer method. Some merely work from Mom's master list until all the chores are checked off. Choose a system that is dynamic and refreshing.

Our family discovered that we made faster progress on some jobs when we removed the loneliness element by pairing up for jobs. Remember that companionship is especially important to the little ones as they collect their toys, arrange their bed pillows, fold the dish cloth, put wild flowers in a small vase, pick the religious music for Sabbath dinner, or some creative duty commensurate to their ages. Songs can be sung, stories told, to make their "Friday preparation education" a time they look forward to.

Recall Deuteronomy 6:6, 7: "[These words] . . . thou shall teach them diligently unto thy children, and shalt talk of them when thou sittest in thine house, and when thou walkest by the way, and when thou liest down, and when thou risest up." May we suggest this also applies to "while working" and getting prepared for the Sabbath?

During one phase in my life, the responsibility of so much preparation for my family on Sabbath in addition to my heavy responsibilities at the university just became too much for me. Burnout was moving into physical problems.

We reorganized ourselves by developing a five-day "to do" list for ourselves and our sons. We also simplified our lifestyle—and what a difference it made. The boys became experts at vacuuming, sweeping the garage, washing the car, and cleaning their rooms, while I finished the shopping, cooking, and the other myriad of details. Father John also had the mowing of the yard, cleaning up his office and other house cleanup jobs to do. We all worked together. If, after all that, teens still have excess energy to burn off before Sabbath, one idea is to send them jogging!

How thankful I was for the help of my sons. They truly became life savers and besides that they learned skills that have helped them to be better husbands today.

Later, when the boys were usually away at school, a student from Bolivia—Delia—came to live with us and helped with the chores in exchange. Now it was Delia who readied our home for the Sabbath, and even cooked some of her special Bolivian dishes. What a relief when she took over the Preparation Day. When I entered the house it smelled so clean with all sorts of delectable aromas floating toward me. First, the baked bread and a favorite potato dish, then on into the living room where I could smell the Lemon Pledge™ furniture polish. Mr. Clean™ all-purpose cleaner announced that the bathroom was sparkling, and to that was added the fragrances of the bath soap and Redken shampoo. And on special occasions a bubble bath was planned especially for Friday afternoon with its fragrance and beautiful bubbles.

Another "Sabbath fragrance" presented itself last Friday when one of my friendly neighbors humorously indicated it was about time for my grass to be cut. The problem was husband, John, was in Mexico. While pushing the mower, I sensed another addition to our Friday bouquet of incense wafting heavenward. The freshly cut lawn an hour before sundown smelled just delightful. Until our tongues are loosed with the language of Canaan, some scents and flavors will never approach description. The mowing experience plus getting the car washed, gassed, and the interior cleaned, added significantly to my insights as to how much credit husbands deserve in the Sabbath preparation process. Husbands, you are needed and appreciated!

In the winter, the scent from the crackling fire in the fireplace indicates it is a special time. In the summer, it is the freshly cut roses that grace the house with their sweet perfume. All these fragrances express a special preparation. I believe that on Friday an exclusive incense wafts heavenward to the throne of our Lord.

This household is ready for the Queen Sabbath, and the Creator, Lord of the Sabbath, signified by the lighting of the Sabbath scented candles. God and His angels must thrill to this incense, and find pleasure in dwelling in a sweet smelling home of order and readiness.

The final incense of the Friday evening is when we turn back the crisp clean sheets, Downy scented, and we are ready to enjoy that delightful unhurried rest of the Sabbath.

There are times we over-extend our plans and take on projects that have too many variables too close to the visit of Queen Sabbath. This challenge is met by gaining a firm, pro-active, control when plans for Friday are still in the embryo stage! Here is our never-will-do-this-again story!

When we began building our family mountain cabin in North Carolina, we felt rushed to get some of the summer projects completed. Son John was in charge of pouring the cement floor, and believed the job could be squeezed in on Friday and finished by sundown. As Friday morning progressed, there were setbacks, and after a quick run down the mountain to get something we forgot at Brevard and a rush back to finish preparing for the cement tuck, we knew that "no way" could we finish before sundown. In this crucial moment we rushed to a neighbors to telephone the concrete company to cancel the trip only to learn that the cement truck was loaded and already on its way up the mountain. We pushed ourselves into a higher gear, and when the unwanted cement truck crawled up our steep driveway, we were close to being ready—but not quite.

As the thick and heavy cement was forced down the shoot, we amateurs discovered how difficult the job to get it to the right spots in the basement. As I watched the father and two sons struggling with the huge mass of substance—that somehow was supposed to be beautifully smooth on top—I knew that never could it be down by sundown. In spite of muscle and sweat, the task seemed impossible. We had taken on more than we should have, and the arriving Sabbath would find us slushing in cement.

In despair, I panicked and retreated to the trailer, for I knew that only God could help us now. I told Him all about our foolish blundering, and pled that He would help us. We were new to the mountain community, and this surely would not be the way to start out sharing our faith in keeping the Sabbath day holy.

I returned to the impossible job, and helped in a limited way while my prayers kept ascending heavenward. Father John kept informing us with a running account of how many more minutes until sundown. The closer we came to that moment, the more encouraged we became that our deadline seemed within our grasp—with the possibility that the job might turn out to be somewhat decent. Father John still carries scars of the battle where the caustic cement sloshed over his boots and burned his legs and there was no time to do anything about it except keep working.

Then came Father's announcement: "Put up your tools; this is good enough. Go down to the stream under the spring hose and take your showers," which incidentally was a cold, shocking experience.

About that moment, the sound of a car was detected bouncing up the hill. "Hi!" greeted our new neighbors, "we just came up to see how you're doing with your cement job!"

All I could do—in mixed exhaustion and praise—was to lift my face to the heavens and silently exclaim, "Thank You, Lord. Thank You for getting us through this Friday disaster."

We didn't set the disaster up on Friday, however. Hindsight tells us that had we actually invaded the Sabbath time with that cement, the Sabbath breaking more likely would have occurred the day we carelessly agreed to do the mammoth job on Friday.

But do we not, in less traumatic ways perhaps, "set ourselves up" for breaking the Sabbath when we allow a series of oversights through the week to "climax" on Friday? Are we looking forward to "meeting the Queen" when we plan the dry cleaning drop-off/pickup for Wednesday/Friday rather than Monday/Wednesday?

Then, oh yes, while we're out, stop at the mall for those forgotten nylons, and then swing by the supermarket to dash in for whipping cream because we just switched our idea about Sabbath dessert. Enough said.

Transmitting the Heritage

We like to believe our sons witnessed with us a life-changing concept of Sabbath planning that day.

Be assured that this intense focus of "getting ready for the Sabbath" can indeed be transmitted. The whole concept was foreign to me when I entered college. I learned from my friends how to prepare for the Sabbath. Little did their moms know when they had role-modeled Sabbath preparation for their girls, long before, that someone like me would be "doing what their daughters did."

How true that "Circumstances may occur to separate the children from their parents and their home, but as long as they live the instruction given in childhood and youth will be a blessing" *(Testimonies,* V1:359). (A discourse on Sabbath keeping precedes this sentence.)

After getting reprogrammed, I liked the new habit with its rewards of being all clean and nicely dressed for Friday evening vespers. Those vespers were refreshing to my soul, as was the sacred music that later floated under my dormitory door from the hallway as I crawled into bed for a good night of rest.

Planning Sabbath Eve (Friday night)

Where the family "comes together for Sabbath" a half hour before sunset to meet—whether around the table or at the piano for Sabbath music or Your Story Hour tape recorder—all depends on the varying sunset times. The goal is to create a Sabbath atmosphere. During the transition time from "preparation day" to "Sabbath Eve," Mom and Dad might begin humming, "Sabbath Is a Happy Day."

Should you ever wish to launch a discussion of lively opinions, venture to ask the question, What kind of supper is the Friday night tradition at your house?

Answers to the traditional Preparation Day meal (everyone claims theirs is the simplest favorite) have included fruit soup, veja-links on buns with

Grandma's fruit cobbler, nothing-but tacos, pea soup containing scrambled eggs (good!), Agape Feast of fruits/nuts/bread, frozen pizza, bean soup and cornbread, rice and applesauce, fruit salad and warm cinnamon rolls, egg salad sandwiches and oatmeal cookies at the lake. These "religious heritage" traditions, like mashed potatoes and apple pie at Grandma's, will make any adult child homesick for the Sabbath again!

Perhaps in all we are saying, you are catching the "flavor" of a conviction that we have. For most Seventh-day Adventists the high celebration of the Sabbath is the Sabbath noon meal. For the Jews it is Friday night sunset and meal. Maybe we have something to learn from them.

In the Jewish community, the onset of Sabbath is celebrated at the evening meal. Accordingly, they bring out their silver, best dishes, nicest tablecloth, and candles. However elegantly simple is your own Friday night traditional meal, it too can be served simply elegant. Two candles, symbolizing Creation and Redemption may be lit, or a candle lit for each member of the family.

In this soothing, comfortable atmosphere, work has ceased. The hour has arrived to peacefully relax, dine, and interface with God and family. Spiritual conversation at any meal during the Sabbath hours may be guided by slips of paper at the plates: "God helped me this week to . . ." "I would especially like God to . . ."

You, too, may choose to linger around the quiet, candlelit table and hold family worship there. Besides reviewing Sabbath School lessons and memory verses for the morning, the family may go over the Scripture reading and hymns to be used in tomorrow's worship hour. A quick call to the church office earlier in the day should elicit this information from the printed bulletins, well worth the effort if your family can delve into, and meditate on, the complete meanings of the selections beforehand.

Your family may continue this Sabbath Eve special time with a new book of family-wide interest purchased earlier in the week for just this moment.

Reasonable early bedtimes on Sabbath Eve will help preserve the Sabbath atmosphere in the morning.

Before retiring, one homemaker completely sets both the breakfast bar for morning and the dining room table for the Sabbath noon meal. On Sabbath, the family—and she herself—feels accepted.

Planning Sabbath Morning (pre-church)

"On Sabbath morning the family should be astir early. If they rise late, there is confusion and bustle in preparing for breakfast and Sabbath School. There is hurrying, jostling, and impatience. Thus unholy feelings come into the home" (*Testimonies,* V1:357).

This past Sabbath I (Millie) was surprised at 9:30 to see so few children present in a Sabbath School division. The leader's response was, "Wait another 20 minutes and the place will be full." I was thus reminded of the challenge of getting children ready and off to church, a job that requires real cooperation from the full family.

The pre-church phase can proceed with sunny dispositions if everyone knows his/her best-suited-for role: fixing a simple breakfast (high-sugar foods not recommended), or clearing breakfast, or dressing younger children, or monitoring the teeth and hair details, or warming up the car. This organization eliminates calling out these concerns to someone two rooms away above the volume of a Sabbath CD.

While Mom and Dad are tending to their "finishing touches" before the family can leave, the rest of the family might listen to a Your Story Hour tape or a story read to them. A subdued atmosphere goes far toward keeping Mom and Dad "collected" so that nothing is overlooked.

Because pre-church disagreements can spoil, and even delay, the trip to Sabbath School, stop and evaluate the situation if this occurs. Reason backward from effect to cause and take the necessary steps to eliminate the problem. This may necessitate a family council.

Special pre-church adventures for "morning persons" might include an early bird walk, followed by a leisurely breakfast outdoors on the patio. As a college student, bird watching on a small rustic bridge with binoculars was my "look forward to" Sabbath event. Just being out in nature with birds singing in the green cathedral was a spiritual blessing. There I ate my breakfast from the brown bag and communicated with God out in his glorious Creation. It did something to my soul.

Planning for Church

Since no one can say it better, here are the words of our friend, Ellen White:

"As you enter the place of worship, ask the Lord to remove all evil from your heart. Bring to His house only that which He can bless. Kneel before God in His temple, and consecrate to Him His own, which He has purchased with the blood of Christ. Pray for the speaker or the leader of the meeting. Pray that great blessing may come through the one who is to hold forth the word of life. Strive earnestly to lay hold of a blessing for yourself" *(Testimonies,* V1:363).

Did you count seven preparatory steps in this paragraph toward receiving your Sabbath blessing in church? Children can also be encouraged to pray for the pastor so that they too might receive a blessing in the worship service.

Planning the Sabbath Meal

Probably at no other time does a homemaker feel more "on trial" than when she opens the front door to her home after church. The moment of truth has arrived. Her family, dressed in their Sabbath finery—bless them—now have taken on the appearance of guests, looking expectantly to see what form of "manna soufflé" today will produce. Can Mrs. Homemaker walk right into a gleaming kitchen, with sparkling windows, straight to the timer oven and refrigerator and immediately place the trivets and crystal on an already laid, beautiful table adorned with fresh flowers?

Mind you, even this scenario may be spoiled if, coming up the driveway, the homemaker sees dandelions in the yard, and then pajamas in the living room. Even if other family members she had depended on had, for very good reasons, been forced to drop the ball, the homemaker sees herself as the one ultimately responsible to handle the alternatives and backup plans—the one looked to for operating the proverbial "well-ordered home." And Sabbath noon is the ultimate test.

Throughout the week, mealtimes and menus may be flexible. But at this moment there is no nagging the family from other activities that "dinner is getting cold." The only thing on their minds now, in this blank space of time between church and dinner, is Mom's nourishment. This is the family moment in which memories are made.

OK. The pressure is on Mrs. Sabbath Homemaker; how does she handle it?

Our daughter-in-law, Ivette, endeavors to prepare for the Sabbath all week so that she and John do not make an exhausting, last minute push on Friday. The duties of laundry and cleaning are spread throughout the week. The Sabbath menu is completed before the weekly grocery shopping. Their plan reminds me of the Old Testament Jews whose focus was always ahead, with each day a march in preparation toward the Sabbath, the climax of what life to them was about.

At times all families are so busy that an exceptionally simple meal—perhaps a gourmet soup, special bread, and an uncomplicated, but hearty salad—can be planned. (The key word is planned.)

May I suggest that even for the simplest meal, lay out the lovely table settings. They were purchased for special occasions; is any occasion more special than the Sabbath? On Sabbath we bring out the wedding dishes, goblets, and best flatware, even if the meal is simple and no guests are present. This deeply influences children that the Guest is present.

Yes, breakage is a risk. I remember being hosted by a pastoral family one Sabbath when the table setting was at its loveliest. Even the children were welcome to drink from the crystal goblets. Then one of the little daughters accidentally broke a goblet as it slipped through her fingers. I always will remember how the mother sweetly comforted her daughter as she cleared away the broken glass and spilled juice.

Some mothers confide, "I'd like to have some friends and children's friends over, but I can't take on more. *Suggestion: Why not have two or three families plan a monthly potluck meal, alternating homes? Friendships will grow, and children will enjoy relation-*

ship time with other children during the Sabbath.

Family Question: What can we do as a family to help the Homemaker with the Sabbath meals and clean up?

Planning Sabbath Afternoon

When our boys were young and very active, we devised a plan: they would give us one hour for reading or napping after our Sabbath meal. We discovered that too much sleep robbed us of a spiritual blessings and time with our sons, besides it broke the sleep cycle making it difficult to go to sleep at bed time. Then, for the rest of the afternoon, we were theirs—for hiking in nature, visiting practically every nature or camping spot within driving distance, playing Bible games, visiting friends, doing good for someone, attending a youth activity, or singing with Dad at the piano, or just talking. Investing Sabbath afternoon with our boys was a part of the family curriculum. It was our relationship time and had high priority.

Planning the Close of Sabbath

We who are borderline workaholics are so tempted to plan more for the Sabbath hours than we should. There has been an early morning committee, Sabbath School, church, a potluck with clean-up detail, rushing to a personal ministries committee, followed by a quick trip back to church for choir practice, then a stop across town, for just ten minutes, to see Brother Alfred who is lonesome in the rest home, and more.

As the sun sinks in the west, we slip into the recliner, exhausted, to have our *family* prayer (but we realize it has not been a *family* day) befor picking up the tasks of a new week with its mile-long "to do" list. We are not the Superworkers we would like to be. God has asked us to "come apart and rest awhile" on the Sabbath Day. Is Sabbath so busy that we look to Sunday to become our day of rest?

Our friend again, Ellen, addresses the close of Sabbath in one sentence, portraying a quiet moment: "As the sun goes down, let the voice of prayer and the hymn of praise mark the close of the sacred hours and invite God's presence through the cares of the week of labor" *(Testimonies,* V1:359).

What will your next Sabbath be like?

Sabbath Preparations Suggested by Ellen White

These suggestions are from *Child Guidance,* pp. 527-537. Some of today's young people may think these suggestions are somewhat old-fashioned; nevertheless, it is beneficial for us to consider the principles behind them and to ask the Holy Spirit how to apply them. How can we joyfully anticipate the Sabbath, with all of its preparation, as well as joyfully experience it?

Friday

- Friday is a preparation day
- Clothing should be ready, cooking completed
- Shoes polished, baths taken
- All regular work is completed or laid aside
- Put away secular books and papers
- Let children share in preparation

Friday evening

- Sabbath opens with Friday sunset worship

- Worship with reading God's Word, prayer and singing
- Put a guard on acts and words

Sabbath morning

- The family should rise early on Sabbath morning
- All should go to worship God
- Be neat and trim without adornment
- Have a special Sabbath suit, clothes

Sabbath dinner

- Food should be simple and less eaten
- Avoid cooking on the Sabbath, food can be warmed
- Provide a special Sabbath treat

Sabbath afternoon

- Plan suitable reading and conversation
- No playing on Sabbath in and out of doors (plan special Sabbath games)
- Take children outdoors to view God in nature
- Devote time to interesting our children
- Close the Sabbath with prayer and songs

True, some of us would like even more "Do and Don't" clarifications, but then, God has given us minds to reason, and the Bible and the Holy Spirit to suggest ways to lighten our choices making the Sabbath a delight. We are all at different levels of Sabbath keeping. The important matter is that we keep focused in the right direction.

Chapter Four

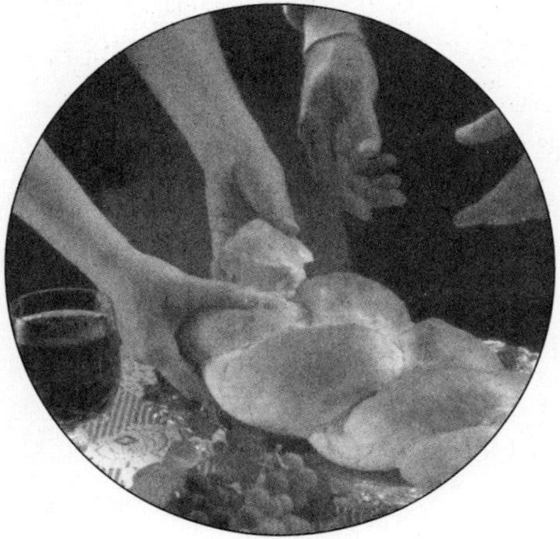

"The seventh day is a palace in time . . ."
(Abraham Joshua Heschel)

The Traditional Jewish Sabbath Revisited

This chapter is background information on the Jewish traditional practice of welcoming the Sabbath. We may gain many insights by revisiting the Jewish customs, but, unlike the Jews, we will not hesitate to make a Christian application and an interpretation of their symbolism based on the New Testament.

The Sabbath ceremony is very important to practicing Jews, for it returns them to their heritage and roots. May-Ellen and Gaspar Colon have researched some of the Jewish practices of their Sabbath rituals and share with us their findings. May-Ellen also interviewed Jacques Doukhan, a professor with a

Jewish background, at Andrews University, and obtained more information on the Sabbath rituals in the Jewish home.

We were further enlightened in our study of transmitting the Jewish religious heritage when we discovered that Richard and JoAnn Davidson celebrate the Jewish rituals in their home on Sabbath. The Davidsons graciously accepted our invitation to share their customs in our home one Sabbath Eve.

Doukhan states that the role of women in Sabbath observance is important. She lights the candles when the Sabbath arrives. Women set the structure of the Sabbath in the family.

Preparing for the Sabbath is as sacred as prayer in Jewish thinking. The women are therefore exempted from certain prayers because they have already prayed in preparing the family for the Sabbath. *Again: preparation for the Sabbath = prayer.*

It was the practice in Jesus' day to announce the stop of all work at the arrival of the Sabbath in Israel by blowing the Shofar horn which is a ram's horn or the horn of an ibex—a wild goat. The priest stood at the southwest corner of the temple mount and blew the horn.

Some skill is required to blow this instrument. When we were in the Cayman Islands we were having difficulty retrieving the right sound from the Shofar horn. The pastor asked, "Let me try," and he successfully blew the horn.

"Wow! How did you do it?" we all asked.

The pastor replied, "It was easy—I play the trumpet."

So, get a trumpet player to give your unique Jewish call to worship!

In Israel, John was able to purchase a Shofar horn for our family, but we are not trumpet players. So the sound is not perfect, but when we try we are reminded that the busy six days of work have ended and that the Sabbath is arriving.

Lighting of the Sabbath Candles

The mother is the queen of the home, and the Sabbath is the Queen of the week. So the wife is the one who leads in the Friday evening sunset worship while the father goes to the synagogue for the traditional service there. He usually arrives home in time for special traditional moments like the blessing of the children, challah bread and grape juice.

Before the Sabbath candles are lit the Jewish mother offers the prayer quoted on pages 60 and 61. Today, in Christian homes, the two candles can represent Creation and Redemption. The idea of candles is taken from Genesis 1:3, 4—at Creation, God said, "Let there be light." Also, Jesus is the Light of the world.

Sometimes Jewish families have more than two candles, one for each member of the family, and guests. Others use a seven-branched candelabra. Another good reason for using candles on Sabbath is that candles are associated with birthdays, and the Sabbath is the birthday of the world.

The effect of such sacred traditions on morale is revealed as a group of Jews was crammed into a train on the way to a Nazi concentration camp. An old Jewish woman had taken with her two Sabbath candles. When she brought them out, Sabbath peace descended on the suffering group. The Sabbath candles transformed a miserable situation. The Sabbath can transform our homes.

The mother also prays a silent prayer for her children, that they may grow up with hearts open to understand and appreciate God's Word. When the father comes home from the synagogue, he blesses the children by taking each one in his arms, or by placing his hands on their bowed heads as he recites a blessing for each child, starting with his sons.

For his sons, he says: "May God make you like unto Ephraim and Manasseh!"

For his daughters: "May God make you like Sarah, Rebekah, Rachel, and Leah!"

Then, for all, the father says: "May the Lord bless you and keep you: May the Lord cause His countenance to shine upon you and be gracious unto you; May the Lord lift up his countenance toward you and give you peace."

Blessings mean a lot to children. In biblical times it was believed that words had power and that what was spoken would happen. Thus Esau asked of his father, "Bless even me, my father." During this time of blessing, there are meaningful touches, hugs, and kisses, the laying on of hands, and affirmation that reinforces in the children who they are and that they are valued by God and by their parents as important members of the family. This touch time is not only for the parents and children but the grandparents as well who still like their hugs.

Characteristics of a blessing:

- Meaningful touches: hugging, kissing, laying on of hands.
- Spoken affirmation.
- Placing high regard upon the person being blessed.

Fathers who wish to enact the Jewish blessing on their children may find word pictures helpful: "You remind me of a . . ." Picture a special future for the one you are blessing. Then make personal commitment to bring about this future.

One helpful approach is to discern a unique

quality of the child's temperament and ask the Lord to take it, and bless it for His service—to be used for His kingdom. For example, a child's sensitivity at present could cause frequent crying spells. But God can develop this sensitivity so the child could become a healer and a leader, one who is able to perceive needs in others.

In addition, the husband reads to his wife Proverbs 31 and blesses her, and the wife may bless her husband.

Challah (pronounced Hallah) Bread

The braided baked bread is called Challah bread. This bread should be fresh baked within 24 hours of Sabbath. In modern Israel you will find this bread only on Thursdays and Fridays. The two loaves symbolize the Bread of Life and the two tables of stone that contained the commandments. They may also symbolize the double portion of manna which was gathered on Friday.

Kiddush

The ceremony of the kiddush (wine) is equivalent to toasting the bride at a wedding. Now the kiddush signals that the Queen, Sabbath, has arrived.

The wine or grape juice symbolizes life. The commandments are life. The juice, as the product of the vineyard, represents that which is alive and nourishing. The ceremony proceeds: Before the blessing of the kiddush, all rise to their feet and repeat: "LICHVOD HASHABBAT—For the glory of the Sabbath!" All then lift up their glasses and repeat: "LECHAIM—To life!"

Sabbath Meal

The Sabbath meal follows. The meal is eaten

leisurely and is served complete with the family's finest china and table covering. For this meal, grace is said after the meal, in accordance with Deuteronomy 8:10: "When you have eaten and are satisfied, you shall bless the Lord your God for the good land which He has given you."

Deuteronomy 8 warns that when everything is going well, the tendency is for hearts to become proud and forget the Lord. I'm surprised how many times we have forgotten to say "thank You" to Him, even after some super dessert. Verse 18 warns, "But you shall remember the Lord God." (Zimmerman, p. 31)

The Friday evening meal is the choicest food of all the week in Jewish homes. Richard Davidson says, "Before each course, someone says, 'For the honor of the Sabbath!' During the meal the family heartily sings joyous table hymns reflecting the feeling and mood of the Sabbath. In the singing, eating, and fellowship the family can forget their weekday burdens, worries, and sorrows." ("The Delight of an Exquisite Day" *Adventist Review,* January 2, 1986, p. 18).

Our Friday evening meals can be special, too. Make them a festive, happy time!

We continue with our reenactment of a Jewish Friday evening ceremony with a group song such as "Shalom Haverim." (See page 64.)

Singing is an important feature of the Jewish Sabbath ceremony. For this, we can sing additional Sabbath eve songs from the hymn book or obtain songs from Messianic Jewish Resources (telephone: 410-358-6471). One song often sung is "Hava Nagila" (sung three times), after which is repeated, "Sabbath is the Queen." Another song is "Shabbat Hamalka," which announces that "Sabbath is here."

An Example

It is not necessary to follow the Jewish traditions exactly and to strictly observe their Friday evening ceremony. Their evening is outlined here as background for Sabbath celebrations in your own family—to stimulate your imagination and help you visualize how Jesus kept the Sabbath. You can adapt these ideas, and may find that although the week has been hurried and troubling, the Friday night blessing can herald a peace that can transform our families today.

These traditions are more than ceremonies, rules, or behaviors. They are an attitude, or frame of mind, that we maintain no matter what the circumstances.

We may thoughtfully wonder whether conducting this type of Friday service, welcoming the Sabbath, would wear out its meaning. Also to contemplate—do these religious ceremonies bear on the fact that there are fewer family breakups in these homes, and that they enjoy closer relationships and loyalties with one another? Do these spiritual traditions influence the transmission of religious heritage and the stabilizing of home in the lives of children and parents?

Challah Bread Recipes

If your family plans to celebrate the Jewish heritage of welcoming the Sabbath, you likely will want to make the Challah bread. If you live in a locality where there is a Jewish bakery, Challah bread can be purchased on Thursday afternoon or on Friday. The recipes we share here, though not exactly authentic, can well serve your family's needs. The dough takes little time to make and can even be prepared in the bread machine. While Challad bread is traditionally made from the finest white flour, some Adventists may wish to use whole-wheat flour to make their own traditional bread.

Basic Hallah Bread (Recipe #1)

(shared by May-Ellen Colon)

- 1/2 cup oil
- 3 teaspoons salt
- 1 tablespoon sugar
- 1 cup boiling water
- 1/2 cup cold water
- 2 packages dry yeast
- 1/3 cup warm water
- 3 eggs, beaten (reserve 1 tablespoon)
- 7 cups unbleached flour

Combine oil, salt, and sugar in a large mixing bowl. Add boiling water and stir. Add cold water. Dissolve yeast in warm water. Add eggs to oil/water mixture, reserving 1 tablespoon beaten egg to brush on the loaves before baking. Add dissolved yeast and stir. Add flour and mix well.

Turn dough out onto floured board and knead until dough does not stick to board or hands. Add more flour if necessary. Return dough to bowl and cover with a clean towel. Place in oven that has been preheated for a moment and then turned off. Let dough rise for one hour or until double in bulk. A hole should remain if poked.

Turn dough out onto lightly floured board again and knead for about a minute. Cut into 12 equal pieces and knead each with a little flour until not sticky. Let dough rest while greasing a cookie sheet with vegetable shortening. Roll each piece of dough into an 8-inch strand. Braid into four loaves.

Place on baking sheet and let rise for 45 minutes at room temperature. Brush tops of loaves with beaten egg. Bake in a 350°F oven for 40 minutes; remove loaves to cooling racks. *Extra loaves may be stored in the freezer.* To restore the fresh flavor to frozen loaves, thaw and place in the oven for 5 to 10 minutes.

Basic Hallah Bread (Recipe #2)

From The First Jewish Catalog, *compiled and edited by Richard Siegel, Michael Strassfeld, and Sharon Strassfeld (Philadelphia: The Jewish Publication Society of America.)*

- 2 cups lukewarm water
- 3 packages yeast
- 8+ cups flour
- 1 1/2 cups sugar, divided
- 1 1/2 teaspoons salt
- 2 sticks (1/2 lb.) margarine or butter
- 5 eggs, beaten (reserve one for glaze)

Combine water and yeast in a very large bowl. Add 3 cups flour and 1 cup sugar. Stir with a fork and let rise 1/2 hour in a warm place.

Meanwhile, measure into another bowl 5 cups flour, salt, and 1/2 cup sugar. Add margarine and cut in with a knife until mixture resembles coarse meal.

After 1/2 hour, add 4 beaten eggs to yeast mixture and stir well. (Mixture will decrease in volume.)

Add flour mixture to yeast mixture and work them together in the bowl. *If sticky, add up to two cups more flour.* Knead well on a floured board until smooth and elastic. Put in an oiled bowl and cover with a towel. Let rise in a warm place for 2 hours or until doubled. Punch down. Knead lightly for a minute or two.

Divide dough: 4 small-medium loaves, 3 medium loaves, 2 large loaves, or 1 huge special wedding loaf.

Braid the loaves and place in oiled loaf pans. Cover and let rise in a warm place for 3 to 4 hours. *Important: the longer you let the dough rise (being careful to not kill the yeast), the lighter will be your loaves.* After dough rises, brush top with reserved beaten egg and bake at 350°F for 45 minutes.

Millie's Challah Bread (Recipe #3)

Just the ingredients are given with a few tips. It turns out a little moist so additional flour may be added. I make the dough in the bread machine which takes a little over 2 hours and 25 minutes.

1 tablespoon yeast + 1 teaspoon sugar
2 tablespoons sugar
1 cup milk or soy milk
1/4 cup butter or margarine
1 teaspoon salt
3 eggs or 3/4 cup EggBeaters®
5+ cups all-purpose flour

To make two braided loaves, each with three strands: place loaves in separate, lightly oiled glass baking dishes. Place each dish over a large pot of water at medium to low heat. Cover each baking dish with a towel. *Usually the dough rises to the desired size in 30 to 45 minutes.* Preheat oven to 350°F; bake 30 to 45 minutes, until the loaves are golden in color. Use a portion of a stick of margarine to lightly glaze the entire top of the loaves, then remove from dishes.

More Information

To obtain a detailed order of the Friday and Saturday evening Jewish services, try this book: *Shabbat: Celebrating the Sabbath the Messianic Jewish Way* by Richard and Michele Berkowitz (Lederer Publications, 410-358-6471). Lederer Publications also has other books, including song books, on the Messianic Jewish theme.

CHAPTER FIVE

"O God of Your people Israel:
You are holy, and You have made the Sabbath
and the people of Israel holy."

(FROM THE CANDLELIGHTING PRAYER OF JEWISH WOMEN)

MODIFYING JEWISH SABBATH CELEBRATIONS

The previous chapter briefly outlined some traditional Jewish practices for Sabbath observance. Now we will note their own adaptations from traditional to contemporary times, and how we may modify the meaningful ceremonies of the Jews to meet our Christian tradition. There is much we can learn from our Jewish friends who have been observing the Sabbath for thousands of years longer than we have.

Should you arrive in Israel early on a Friday afternoon, you would observe the streets bustling with shoppers, laden with beautiful flowers, returning home. On every street corner you would see vendors selling these flowers as centerpieces for Sabbath tables. All seem to be rushing with a purpose in mind.

Then, could you slip into one of the homes of the observant, Orthodox Jews, you would find them—still early in the afternoon—with their Sabbath preparation completed, getting out their Tanach (Old Testament). Husband and wife would open it to the Song of Songs and read together.

The Sabbath is a time of great intimacy between the bride and Groom, with Israel as the bride and God Himself as the Groom. And so, long before sunset, begins the special fellowship between the bride and Groom, with the Song of Songs striking the note of intimacy.

Also quite some time before sundown (no pushing the workweek to the "last minute" here!) the Shofar horn is blown, announcing that the Sabbath is arriving and calling for a celebration. Unlike Jesus' day, when a ram's horn or an ibex (wild goat) horn, was blown, today an electronic imitation is used. Nevertheless, its sound induces a mood of joy, because the Sabbath—more than anything else—is a time of joy for the people of Israel.

Sabbath songs, such as Shabbat Hamalka, often announce the grand entrance of the Sabbath queen.

A Sacred Party

The Sabbath is a day for holy celebration, not to be overshadowed by "legalism" in Christian homes. This does not mean that the Sabbath is to be celebrated like a party. However, after we had officiated a Jewish-style Sabbath celebration in the Cayman Islands, a young boy named David who had participated with his family, called the experience "like having a sacred party." This was all right, he reasoned, because we were celebrating the birthday of the world. He happily concluded, "We can do this every week!"

Abraham Joshua Heschel calls it a sin to be sad on the Sabbath day. If Sabbaths are not a happy day, our children may choose to outgrow the fourth commandment as they outgrow childhood.

Using, Adapting, Jewish Traditions

In our home, we like to play these happy Jewish songs as Sabbath guests arrive. We also like to light the Sabbath candles on Sabbath Eve (one representing Creation, the other Redemption—here adapted to symbolize the Cross). We serve grape juice in crystal glasses (a symbol of "life" to the Jews, adapted here to symbolize the blood of Christ) and bread (a symbol of "manna" to the Jews, adapted here to symbolize the body of Christ). Then we do our own reading and praying. If other guests or children are present, we sometimes add more elements of the celebration.

The full service, as we have come to understand it, is basically as follows, with any portion to be adapted or omitted as meets your preference and time.

We humbly submit here the fruit of our passionate research. We have presented this material at Loma Linda, California, at various Family Life Seminars and conferences, and have adapted them for family worship in the home. Every group, we learn, personalizes the procedure.

Sabbath Celebration Program

Songs:

"Come to Worship" (p. 112)
"Welcome, Welcome, Sabbath Day" (p. 114)
"Hevenu Shalom Aleichem" (p. 116)

Sharing:

Sabbath is God's day, and ours. For twenty-four

hours, God's people in different time zones around the world welcome the Sabbath into their homes.

Songs:

"Shabbat Hamalka/Queen Sabbath" (p. 118)
(The Sabbath Is Almost Here)
"Dear Lord, We Come at Set of Sun"
(SDA Hymnal, #392)

The Call:

Someone blows the Shofar horn, if possible.
Or a recording of it is played, if obtainable.

Invitation:

Prayer of Jewish women, before lighting the candles, to invite the Queen (Sabbath), into the home:

"O God of Your people Israel:
You are holy,
and You have made the Sabbath
and the people of Israel holy.
You have called upon us to honor the Sabbath
with light,
with joy and with peace—
As a king and queen give love to one another;
as a bride and her bridegroom—
So have we kindled these two lights for love of
Your daughter, the Sabbath.
Almighty God, Grant me and all my loved ones
a chance to truly rest on this Sabbath day.
May the light of the candles drive out from among
us the spirit of anger, the spirit of harm.
Send Your blessings to my children,
that they may walk in the ways of
Your Torah, Your Light.
May You ever be their God, and mine, O Lord,
my Creator and my Redeemer.
Amen."

Candlelighting:

The mother lights the two Sabbath candles:

One candle to symbolize Creation, the birthday of the world. All say as candle is lit: "Remember the Sabbath."

One candle to symbolize Redemption, adapted to the cross. All say as candle is lit: "To keep it holy."

The Command:

Repeat the Sabbath commandment in Exodus 20:8-11.

Mother's Prayer:

The mother offers a silent prayer for her children that they may reach adulthood with hearts open to understanding and appreciating God's Word.

Song:

"Sabbath Blessing" (or read words) p. 117

Father's Blessing:

"Will all the children please come forward and kneel around me?"

Prayer for sons: "May God make you like unto Ephraim and Manasseh!

Help *(son's name)* to reach the highest goals in his life. Bless *(other son's name)* so that he will be all he can be. May he ever stand tall for Your truth, and stand for the right—no matter what others may say or do."

Prayer for daughters: "May God make you like Sarah, Rebekah, Rachel, and Leah! As you grow into womanhood, may you be a blessing to others like Ruth and Queen Esther."

Add personalized blessings for each child.

For family: "May the Lord bless you and keep you,

May the Lord cause His face to shine upon you and be gracious unto you; May the Lord lift up His countenance toward you and give you peace.

Touch Time:

During this time there can be hugs and kisses and touching, which can include the grandpa and grandma who may be skin hungry and appreciate the loving caresses and spoken affirmation of their family.

Father Blesses Mother:

"Who can find a virtuous wife?
For her worth is far above rubies.
The heart of her husband safely trusts her,
She looks well to the ways of her household,
And does not eat the bread of idleness.
Her children rise up and call her blessed'
Her husband also, and he praises her, saying:
'Many daughters have done well, but you excel them all.'
A woman who fears the Lord, she shall be praised." (Proverbs 31:10-31, shortened version)

Family Song:

The family sings together a blessing for each.
(First point out that the empty chair is for Jesus.)

"Bless Our Home" *(sing to the tune of "Edelweiss")*
Bless our home, bless our food;
Come, O Lord, and sit with us;
May our talk glow with peace,
May Your love surround us;
Friendship and love, may they bloom and grow,
Bloom and grow forever;
Bless our home, bless our food;
Come, O Lord, and sit with us.

Source: *Celebrate the Feasts* by Martha Zimmerman. Minneapolis: Bethany House Publishers, 1981, p. 38.

Serve:

Distribute small glasses of grape juice. Pass a loaf of bread from which each person pulls off a piece.

Share:

The kiddush is the prayer of sanctification of the wine. The hamotzi is the blessing of the bread. We have the wine and challah bread to enjoy together. The kiddush is equivalent to toasting the bride at a wedding. Here we honor the Queen, Sabbath, Who has come to visit us.

All say: "LICHVOD HASHABBAT—For the glory of the Sabbath!"

All lift glasses and say, "LECHAIM!—To Life!" *With joy, all drink the grape juice.*

The bread symbolizes manna, the Bread of Life. Prayer: "HAMOTZI!"—Blessed art Thou, O Lord our God, King of the universe, who brings forth bread from the earth." *With joy, all eat the bread.*

Sabbath Eve Meal:

In many Sabbath-keeping homes, the Sabbath Eve meal is an Agape feast which includes choice fruits and nut breads. In Jewish homes, traditional Jewish songs are sung. In Seventh-day Adventist homes, songs from the hymnal, concerning the Sabbath, may be sung.

Song:

"Shalom Haverim"

Shalom haverim, shalom haverim, shalom, shalom.
L' –hit-ra-ot, l-hit'ra'ot, shalom, shalom.

Shalom, my friends, shalom, my friends,

Shalom, shalom.
May peace be with you, God's peace be with you,
Shalom, shalom.

May blessings attend you, angels defend.
Shalom, shalom.
God's mercies befriend you unto the end.
Shalom, shalom.

Till we meet again, till we meet again,
Shalom, shalom.
May God be with you, His peace be with you.
Shalom, shalom.

Potential Items Needed for Jewish Sabbath Celebrations

Setting: the whole family is present in Sabbath—but not formal—apparel. The wife often wears a white dress. The family is seated, with an extra, empty chair symbolizing the presence of Jesus.

Gasper and May-Ellen Colon, who frequently conduct Sabbath seminars in the Jewish way, have listed the items needed for these services.

Sabbath Eve sunset worship:

- Piano and sheet music, or a Power Point computer program with songs on slides
- Overhead projector or a Power Point computer program to show transparencies
- Handouts of materials
- CD or cassette player for background music before beginning
- Pair of candle holders
- Two white candles and matches
- Goblets and grape juice
- One or two loaves of Challah bread. Serve on a tray or in a basket lined with a napkin

- Napkins
- Bible, with notes
- A special dinner, if possible, after the Sabbath welcoming—this is dependent upon the sunset hour and meal schedule
- For the table: a pure white tablecloth, special dishes, flowers
- Shofar horn or a tape of one blown

Sabbath evening worship:

- Incense or potpourri
- Candle
- Spice box of bassamen

A Religious Heritage

One may ask, understandably, the effort involved, is it worth it?

Let us share with you the reward we received from two young guests, ages six and nine, who participated in these worship activities in our home. I (John) took the children as would a Jewish father, and blessed them, asking God that they might grow up like Rachel, Leah and Rebekah.

Their little hearts were touched. The girls returned home to Pennsylvania and decided that they, too, would welcome the next Sabbath in this unique way. Because their mother worked in the medical world, she did not arrive home at sundown as she had intended. While waiting for her, the girls planned their own Sabbath evening worship service, adapting it in their childlike ways. Mary and Julie sat down in the living room with glasses of grape juice, bread and began to thank Jesus in prayer for what was on their young hearts.

The sun had gone down and the room was darkened. While praying Mary was impressed to open her eyes—the room seemed radiant with an unusual light. She closed her eyes and prayed more. Opening her eyes again—the room was still full of unusual light. As though it was too much for her alone, she called out, "Julie, open your eyes." The sight of the strange light frightened them and both closed their eyes again and prayed. When their prayers were over both opened their eyes again to the twilight darkness that surrounded them. They shared this unusual experience with Uncle Mark who related it to us.

As the family meditated on this strange event they came to the conclusion that God is pleased when even little children are prepared to meet with Him at the appropriate time which He designated as "hallowed."

A Personal Testimony

The following beautiful story comes from our friend, Gerty Thorpe. She tells us: "Some time ago a missionary family home on furlough had been staying with me a while. The departure plan was to leave on Friday to cover a good distance of the twenty-four hour drive to the airport.

"From early morning, complications kept arising, and one could feel the tension escalating among the family. Adding to the irritations of unaccomplished goals and weariness of packing, was the hot weather. The question of departure progressed from agreement to debate. By early evening they announced that traveling was put off till Sunday.

"At my request, the family agreed to join me for sunset worship. But with great reluctance, for the couple were at odds with each other and emotionally separated.

"'Lord,' I pleaded, 'as we welcome Sabbath tonight, please give me wisdom from above how to lead these dear ones into the rest and peace You promised.'

"God, in His faithfulness, brought to my mind a Sabbath evening I had spent with a family who celebrate and welcome Sabbath in the Jewish tradition. A first time experience, it had left a delightful, deep impression on me.

"The mother complied with my request to come to the piano and sing. Her beautiful hymns penetrated the house. Soon the rest of the family gathered around. She then lighted the candles, as I asked, and said a prayer welcoming the Sabbath, coveting blessings for her children from the God of Israel according to Jewish tradition.

"I then asked her husband to bless his four children. He recognized their uniqueness, their qualities, and each individual's accomplishments that week. And then, he blessed his wife also!

"Oh, what warmth and joy was felt in my home that Friday evening. I saw the eyes of their children light up as they were melting into embraces of love and affirmation from Mom and Dad, feeling their security of worth and unconditional love—acting as Jesus' true representatives, doing what Jesus would do.

"Later the father expressed to me that he believes the Lord allowed all the difficulties of that day to keep them there. 'I needed to be reminded of the value of my family,' he said. 'I have neglected to bless and affirm my wife and children. Thank you for reminding me that my first mission is to my family, above going to the uttermost parts of the world! I needed to learn this all over again, before going back to the field of service. I will celebrate the Sabbath in this way from now on.'

"Thanks be to God, Who blessed the Sabbath and hallowed it!" Gerty concludes.

Every Sabbath Eve, somewhere, most of these individuals: the two girls; David (boy in the Cayman Islands); Richard and JoAnn Davidson; Gaspar and May-Ellen Colon; Brooks and Susan Payne; Gerty Thorpe, and we Youngbergs, are celebrating David's "sacred party" of the birthday of the Creator's world.

Would you like to join us?

Small Group Activity

Discuss:

- What is this experience saying to me?
- What are the Christian connotations?
- How can we apply these Jewish Sabbath traditions we have witnessed?
- Was the experience a celebration?

Chapter Six

"Your Story Hour was another favorite that was saved just for Friday night . . . . we would lie down on the living room rug together and listen to the beloved voices of Aunt Sue and Uncle Dan."

(Bonnie Duerksen Norton)

Special Sabbath Memories

Since the goal is to make the Sabbath a joyful and memorable experience, one must think creatively what the family can do to make it so.

It seems that the Father God wants our children to grow in happy Sabbath experiences from early childhood. The earthly father and mother take part in making God's will done by planning the Sabbath Day appropriate for the age level of the children. It is a day for the family to commune, with God, one another, and nature.

Bonnie Duerksen Norton shares with us some of her pleasant memories of the Sabbath when growing up in the mission field. The Duerksen family were neighbors to the Youngbergs in Bolivia when Bonnie was a little girl. Now she is married to Bill and has two precious, vibrant daughters who also enjoy the Sabbath so much that they start the Friday Sabbath celebration time earlier than sundown.

Bonnie says: “As long as I can remember, my only Sabbath memories are positive and special. I do not ever remember resenting the Sabbath as a child or teenager. God was always the central focus in our family and we faithfully observed morning and evening worship.

“But several things made Friday evening worship different and special from the rest of the week. First, we had the entire series of Uncle Arthur’s Bedtime Stories. We loved those books. We were not allowed to read them during the week, only on Friday evening and Sabbath. I was a bookworm and I just could hardly wait for the Sabbath to arrive so I could devour those books.

“Your Story Hour audio tapes were another favorite that was saved just for Friday night. That was back before you could buy the set for yourself. We had the reel-to-reel tape recorder. Apparently we could rent Your Story Hour reels, because I remember they had to be sent back. We would all lie down on the living room rug together and listen to the beloved voices of Aunt Sue and Uncle Dan. Again, an absolute highlight of the week. Later, we bought the records.

“To start worship, we would always sing ‘Day Is Dying in the West.’ To close worship we would form a circle, hold hands, and Daddy would lead out in prayer with his rich, deep, bass voice. I love his voice!

“After prayer, everybody would go around the circle, hugging and kissing everybody else and wishing everybody a Feliz Sábado. After worship we would have a special Friday night supper, usually fruit salad, cinnamon rolls, and hot chocolate.

"Mamma always fixed extra food for Sabbath lunch, always a treat. It was the only time in the week that we ate dessert. And we had a special drink, as well. Back in those days individual church families would invite any visitors home for lunch. Now we leave it all up to a potluck committee. I really miss that personal touch. We never knew who would be coming home for lunch, but it seems like more often than not, somebody would grace our table.

"After a short rest time following lunch, we would always go do something together as a family. In Bolivia I remember walking out to the villages to do branch Sabbath Schools. Here in the States we would visit parks, fish hatcheries, the local zoo, or just go on long hikes. Often, when we would hike together, Dad would bring a book along, and when we were all tired, we would flop down in some grassy spot and he would read to us. I guess for me, the word "Sabbath" just brings up warm, happy, fuzzy feelings of family and love.

"My husband, Bill, grew up with basically the same traditions. So when we got married, we resolved to carry these on. Of course there were slight variations. His family always ate rice and applesauce (they called it 'happy sauce') every Friday evening. So now our Friday night tradition is rice, applesauce, sweet rolls, and hot chocolate.

"His family always sang, 'O'er the Hills the Sun Is Setting.' Now we sing, 'Day Is Dying in the West,' on Friday night and 'O'er the Hills the Sun Is Setting' on Sabbath night. This way we both are able to pass on some of our childhood traditions to our children. I firmly believe that traditions give our children a sense of identity and security.

"Preparation for the Sabbath is almost as special as

the Sabbath itself. Yes, it is work, but getting the house sparkling clean from top to bottom is such a good feeling. There comes a real feeling of peace when everyone has had their bath, the house is clean, and the food all cooked for the next several meals. Now we all can just relax and enjoy time out with one another and with Jesus.

"We have a special Sabbath rug, a huge Alpaca rug that we bought when we lived in Peru that covers the whole living room. It is so soft. After all the other work is done, we vacuum the floor, using nice smelling powders that fill the house with a nice, fresh smell. Then I let the girls lay out the Sabbath rug. They love to snuggle down in this rug and read or color.

"About a half hour before Sabbath begins, I put on our Sabbath music. These are all the old Heritage Singers CDs that Bill and I grew up with. They bring back very warm memories for us. We save these CDs only for Sabbath.

"We all take our Sabbath baths, even those of us like me who prefer a bath in the morning. There is just something special about starting Sabbath with our home, our bodies, and our hearts clean. Then we get into our pajamas.

"I always decorate the Friday night table really pretty. I have made place mats with matching napkins to go with every season and holiday of the year, and I lay the table accordingly."

Family Activity

What are some of your Sabbath memories as a family? Which ones include those memories of Dad and Mom and Grandpa and Grandma?

Chapter Seven

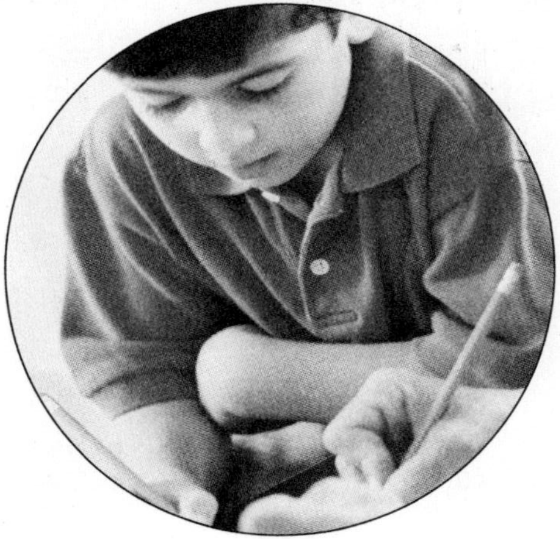

"The Sabbath—oh!—make it the sweetest, the most blessed day of the week. . . ."

(Child Guidance, p. 532)

Sabbath at Church

The captivating Sabbath School program that the children's leaders have used to channel their wiggles and energy has come to a close. Now it is time for the transition from intriguing activities to quiet worship in the sanctuary. This calls for a "transition" mood. Some parents take their little ones for a little stroll between Sabbath School and church.

Making the worship hour special for the children was a challenge for this Grandma and Grandpa. The children's story helped, but then there was the sermon time as well.

When you observe some families coming to church loaded with a trunk-size bag of books, games, cheerios, crunchies, and crumbling crackers, you know they are trying to meet the challenge. It is all ammunition to keep the children happy for one hour of church time. Some parents "overdo" it, while others might benefit by a little flannel board box with felts, or a soft toy, or a book with buttons to button and zippers to open and close. It is usually helpful to give the child one item at a time.

Hint: attach a piece of yarn to the items so that mom, dad, or seat partners are not bending to pick up the toy again and again. Otherwise it can become a game: "Mommie, pick up."

When our granddaughter, Jenny, was small, Grandma drew a picture of Jenny, and Jenny drew a picture of Grandma in her Sabbath dress. Another positive drawing possibility is to have the child draw a scene from the children's story and an illustration from the sermon. That is what Esther Knott's father encouraged her to do when she was a child and now Olivia her daughter does the same. In the beginning, children may need some help regarding ideas, but, once stimulated, their idea skills will improve. If there are stained glass windows that tell a story, they may wish to draw what they see. Esther Knott has just prepared a coloring book for Pioneer Memorial Church children of the stained glass windows and the story behind them. You might be able to do the same at your church. Always keep some paper and crayons available for such an activity and then share after the pictures: "Tell me about your picture."

Recently during church, I was impressed by a family in front of us. The children knew all the words to the hymns and sang out heartily. Then, as they were sitting quietly, I stole a glance at what was keeping them occupied. I saw words on a grid: God-Jesus-love-sin-commandments-forgive-wow-Sabbath-kind and others. I discovered that when the minister used these words, they were recorded. The girls were listening intently to the message, and, hopefully, they were absorbing more from the sermon than isolated words and the number of times they were repeated.

Others, besides parents and grandparents, help us meet the "quiet" challenge. We were delighted when our grandchildren discovered that by visiting the hostess desk they were handed an interesting, spiritual activity sheet called the "Children's Worship Bulletin" they could fill out during the sermon, which they did enjoy. One sheet is directed to ages three to six, another for those seven to twelve.*

Young Stewardship

A special moment in children's spiritual development during the worship hour is the big moment the offering plate is passed. This moment is especially meaningful if the child has earned the money herself/himself.

Tari Pop relates that she had given her daughter, Lauren just the appropriate amount of money for her school clothes. While driving to town, Tari and Lauren thought about the fact that Lauren, only nine, could pay tithe on this money. Lauren agreed, knowing full well that she might not then have enough money for her clothing items. Then (the wonder of it all!), Lauren volunteered to also give some of the money as offering—directly from her "shopping kitty."

Lauren was blessed beyond expectation, for Tari and Lauren found the clothes she needed all on sale.

*These most helpful materials did lend to greater reverence in the House of God and are available from:
2000 Communication Resources, Inc. 4150 Belden Village Street, 4th floor Canton, Ohio 44718 1-800-992-2144

The total for tithe, offering, and clothing came out right to the penny! After this experience, can anything on earth below unsettle this child's conviction that "He who is for us is greater than He who is against us"? What a precious aspect of transmitting religious heritage would have been lost had there not been the "mother-daughter talk" on the way to town!

Disruptive Moments

Don't despair. Seize the moment a child begins to be disruptive as an opportunity to teach reverence for the House of God. Should you have to take a child out, it is important that the child be returned to the service. This prevents the child from the notion that misbehaving has its rewards—he/she will not have to remain in church for the full service. Better that the child be deprived of a Sabbath treat at noon, or a similar reinforcement.

Again, taking a child for a walk between Sabbath School and church can release pent-up energy and ease the child from the happy interaction in Sabbath School into a calmer frame reference for the upcoming worship hour.

Follow-up

A nice tradition at the Sabbath noon meal is a family dialogue on the meaning of the worship hour while it is fresh in mind. Inquire what, from the sermon made the deepest impression on their memory. Did they grasp the main point of the message? Discuss these points on the appropriate level of the children's understanding. Or, summarize for them the "bottom line." Repeat the summary during sunset worship to "lock in" the guiding principle for the coming week.

The young listeners will come to anticipate these

two questions Sabbath noon, and listen with a purpose in mind. Let them catch the idea that for adults something very meaningful is going on here, something that will unfold to them with time. Give them appetizers now, with the assurance that the full meal will come. Have them to understand that the sermons are deeply meaningful to adults and that as they advance in birthdays, they will grow to understand why. For now, "the guiding principle of today's sermon to take with us into the new week is . . ." Brainstorm with the child some potential situations in which this principle can improve her/his life in the upcoming week.

Chapter Eight

Sabbath Afternoon Activities

"How can children receive a more correct knowledge of God, and their minds be better impressed, than in spending a portion of their time out-of-doors, not in play, but in company with their parents?"

(Child Guidance, p. 534)

Merlyn, who I had watched grow from a young boy into a mature young college student, was traveling across the state with me. Merlyn was the son of a pastor who was also the president of a conference. As the miles and hours of our trip passed, Merlyn shared his spiritual journey with me.

One bit of the conversation I will never forget. Merlyn shared, "I have asked myself, Why do I pay tithe and keep the Sabbath and the rest of God's commandments? I had to reflect on this for some time, and then concluded that the only reason was because I love Jesus."

Six months later, Merlyn was killed in an auto accident. What a comfort it was to the parents to hear again of their son's commitment and love for his Jesus.

Merlyn had related His love for Jesus with his keeping the Sabbath. Surely Merlyn's parents had developed in him that it took a God of love to give him such a gift of love.

The purpose of this chapter is to make this gift of love so real to our children that after Sabbath dinner, the next thing to look forward to is not sundown and "getting on" with friends and fun. Family time, perhaps with some friends included, can be just as joyful a time. Let's plan!

Out In Nature

When we look back into the memory book of the Youngberg family, some of the special Sabbath times come to mind as important. There were the weekend camping trips to Baldwin, Michigan—no comfort facilities, but lots of fresh air! These weekends were so enjoyable we encouraged other families with children our age to join us there for the Sabbath (and then canoeing down the Pierre Marquette River on Sunday). What fun that was for all the families.

Other times neighborhood teens joined us also as we tromped through the woods at Love Creek Nature Center—with a few happy pranks along the way—to see how many birds we could identify. Other times they might join us for a Bible study on the last days of Earth's history.

When camping out over Sabbath, the "A to Z" scavenger hunt wonderfully stimulates new awareness of beauty in nature. These "finds" lead to lasting spiritual benefits, especially when the discoverer thinks of a spiritual lesson to share for the object or creature.

Nature has something for everyone. The toddler squeals with excitement when a squirrel darts in front of them, and the teen suddenly identifies a new warbler never seen before.

There is something renewing about checking out the vines on the trees, studying the pure beauty of the water lily in the dirty pond, identifying the bird songs, feeling the gentle rain, hearing the crashing thunder alternate with the lapping of waves along the sturdy rocks on the shoreline.

Have you noticed that families out together in nature seem to be drawn closer to each other as well as to God? It is advised that "the family that camps together, stays together." Nature anywhere stimulates thoughtful questions and curiosity of the family. Knowledge is stored, and personal spirituality enhanced.

Children are naturally creative, driven by an energy flow. If launched, they will spin off on many original and positive Sabbath activities. One challenge to them is a Bible-nature mural or collage. Pick a Bible story, and read it to refresh the memory and meaning. Then, on the grass or in the sand, depict the story with sticks, stones, shells, coral. Divide the different scenes by a stick or arch in the sand, with perhaps a different family member working on the scene beside it. If the subject is kept secret, the family has fun guessing when through. Delightful activities like these, however, do make the Sabbath pass too quickly!

Some families get yearly memberships at zoos so they can go any Sabbath. Long walks "zooing" around, followed by a picnic lunch, makes for a great late Sabbath afternoon. After a while, of course, we've learned that a family can get "zooed out," so, let the brainstorming continue here.

There were Sabbaths that it seemed God just couldn't wait to show us His surprises out in real nature. We considered how disappointed He would have been had we stayed inside that day.

Once He inspired some baby raccoons to follow us down a path, and next they tried to climb a small tree with a crooked trunk—right in our close-up view. How we all wanted to take them home, but we knew that was not wise.

There have been some real shows by Canadian geese. We have watched the little goslings be protected by Mom and Dad. One parent led the little guys across the road with the other parent bringing up the rear. When they rest on the bank they are also protected on both sides by a parent. What a touching example! The grandchildren love to feed the geese, who seem most thankful for day-old bread and choice seeds.

"I spy God!" was our recognized outcry that one of us in the family had spotted in nature something exciting or unusual. We were holding worship on the shore of Lake Chapin early one morning, when we heard unusual sounds in the lake. Looking up, we saw what seemed hundreds of fish mouths open at the water's edge, feeding on the top of the water.

There was the old hollow tree the boys loved to climb from within, and with broad grins announce their feat from the top. We walked the beaches, rode bikes through the cornfield, would swing on the strong grape vines, go "birding," visit nature centers, canoe down a peaceful river, climb the sand dunes and hold evening worship on the top as the sun sank into Lake Michigan. Never to be forgotten was the special sunset moment when from the dunes we watched the fiery red ball sink into the lake while within it were silhouetted the skyscrapers of Chicago some 60 miles away including what at that time was the highest building in the world.

Suggested Nature Activities

1. Find something outdoors as a spiritual object lesson and see if the family can find a text that refers to it.
2. After a Sabbath walk, write a letter to a relative or friend, including what you saw, investigated, compared, or liked most.
3. Follow animal tracks and study the habitat of the animal.
4. Bring extra food on your Sabbath picnic meal to feed ducks, fish, or chipmunks.
5. Choose a Sabbath collection hobby: leaves, flowers, or rocks.
6. Discover one thing new in nature to call to the attention of the family.
7. Take an early Sabbath morning bird walk and record those sighted.
8. Take a solitary walk in nature, and meditate on God's greatness and praise Him for His blessings.
9. When the moon is full, take a Friday evening walk on the beach or in the woods.
10. Enjoy supper and worship by a campfire or on a quiet beach.

En route some special nature spot, the family can play made-up Bible games that require no materials to tote. An easy example is "I'm thinking of a Bible name that begins with 'A' and continue through the alphabet until you arrive at the nature spot.

Suggested names:

Abel	Obadiah
Bathsheba	Peter
Cain	Queen of Sheba
David	Rachel
Enoch	Samson
Festus	Timothy
Gideon	Uriah the Hittite
Hannah	Vashti
Isaac	Woman at the well
Jesus	Xerxes (technically Artaxerxes)
Korah	(Rich) Young Ruler
Lot	Zacchaeus
Mary	
Noah	

After all the abundant energies of the boys had been put to the strain in these nature outings, they were more restful.

Many wonderful family memories linger. And remember, nature outings are enjoyed both cross-gender and cross-generational.

"Doing Good"

During the summer interim between high school graduation and beginning Union College, I held a secretarial job. Another lady in the office had a terminally ill daughter, and she inquired whether I might go sit with her daughter in the hospital sometime when she needed help.

I chose Sabbath as the day to sit with my new friend's daughter. I felt so helpless, but at least I was present if assistance was needed. No miracle happened for the young lady, in her late twenties, but a miracle of love did fill my heart for this young stranger.

Although we talked little, she did manage to smile

sweetly as I left, and say, "You were an angel in pink." I had worn my prettiest, "happy" pink dress for this hospital visit.

She passed away a few days later. I had had the privilege of ministering to her on the Sabbath. Jesus, my Example, when He was here, ministered to the sick. Miracles occurred then, too, like the miracle of love in my heart that day. When we minister, do you think the healing may be in our own lives?

Doing good on Sabbath could also include helping newly baptized members by mentoring them. We might show them Sabbath observance by including them in our Sabbath Eve worships, early morning bird walks, the Sabbath noon meal, and Sabbath afternoon activities right through to vespers or sunset worship. One young new believer enjoyed this experience of Sabbath celebration with a "seasoned" family so much that she joyfully told her unbelieving father that it was the best day of her life!

And then, it may indeed be our own children who need the role-modeling of Sabbath observance, especially if the family is new at Sabbath keeping.

Ask your family to read Matthew 12:12, and ask each person to think of some "do good" activity appropriate for Sabbath and how it can be implemented. The list you create may look something like this:

1. Take a flower basket, loaf of bread, or some other treat to a widow, someone ill or handicapped, or a discouraged person.

2. Adopt a grandparent at a local nursing home and think of ways to bring happiness to this person.

3. Invite home after church a single parent or someone who comes to church alone for dinner and Bible games.

4. Share Insights, Guides, and storybooks with friends in the neighborhood.
5. Volunteer to baby-sit so that some overworked mother may take a walk or a break.
6. Read to a blind person. This is a pleasure for children learning to read, as well as for the one read to.
7. Invite neighbors to enroll in the Voice of Prophecy Correspondence Course.
8. Take the Sabbath sermon tape to a shut-in.
9. Share promises with someone who needs encouragement by calling or writing.
10. Plan, arrange, and implement a special program for a nursing home, sometimes called "Sunshine bands."
11. Write letters for an elderly person to one of her/his relatives. Perhaps reread to the person letters already received.
12. Find a junior devotion story and read it to a non-member neighbor, perhaps one playing outside.
13. Make someone a love gift.
14. Write texts or quotes on a 5x8 card, and design or illustrate it for a discouraged person.
15. Print mottos (e.g., "My boss is a Jewish carpenter.") on long strips of tag board for a person needing encouragement. Include two decorative magnets with each in order to be displayed among the refrigerator art.
16. Go to Grandma and Grandpa's house to be read a story.

At-home Sabbaths

Sometimes it is impossible to go to a lovely park. This was the case with Erma and her two primary-age children because Grandpa needed care. But Erma did have a lovely back yard, and the children discovered the fun of a magnifying glass. They searched the grass and flower bed for tiny, creepy-crawlies. They inspected the intricate beauty of a small, insignificant leaf, or little flower. They invented a game to see who could discover the most interesting "live" things in the back yard.

Some other activities for those who are "in" for Sabbath may include:

1. Take plain white paper placemats and personalize and decorate with Sabbath scenes for the family's evening meal, or even for next Sabbath's dinner guests and Grandma and Grandpa.

2. Search out angel stories* and read one to your family. Then ask one family member to retell the story in her/his own way, using sanctified imagination. The creativity employed will induce smiles and laughter. The truism, "that which you give, you keep," surely applies to storytelling as memory skills are developed.

3. Ask one family member to begin a story and stop at some point. Someone else picks up the story, and likewise stops. This continues until someone concludes the story. Angel stories may

---

***Books of angel stories:** *Walking With Angels* by E. Lonnie Melashenko; *An Angel's Touch* by Natalie Lader-Bischoff; *In the Presence of Angels* by E. Lonnie Melashenko; available at your local Adventist Book Center.

be used here also. A good source is *Story of Redemption,* by Ellen White.

4. Choose a Bible story to read. Then ask one person to serve as the reporter, as though actually at the scene and reporting the event live. Or, report the story from the perspective of a character in the story.

5. Dramatize a spiritual truth, and ask family members to identify the point. For example, create an airplane scenario (even stuffed animals may be the passengers, with designated "voice over" animations). Passengers alternate complaints: pilot is going the long way, pilot isn't flying high enough; pilot is dumb the way he's approaching the storm, etc., until passengers defiantly take over the cockpit. (Do we trust Jesus, our Pilot—or do we try to "take over"?)

6. Make bookmarks by pressing a wildflower or beautiful leaf between two pieces of clear contact paper, a nice gift for children to give elderly persons with whom they can read from the Bible or Ellen White about leaves.

7. Make cards of encouragement to send the bereaved or ill.

8. At Christmas, each family member chooses one figurine from the nativity scene and tells the story as if she/he were there. Or, the Luke account may be read, with each person participating as her/his figurine appears in the narrative.

9. Children may make a small book for a child in the hospital, with artsy covers made from extra wallpaper or contact paper. Book may contain poems, promises, pictures.

10. Musical or imaginative children may find a chapter in the Bible and work at giving the words their own spontaneous melody. The words will be wallpapered in their memory.

11. Start a Personal Memory Notebook for each child. Identify the meaning of the child's name, and study the Scriptures to see if it appears. If so, write the character's story in the notebook.

    In other sections, record a list of birds (or wild flowers or trees) spotted, including where and when. Record prayer requests with the date answered, and how it was answered, in red. Write Thank You beside each answer. Draw pictures in the book of how God blessed or answered the prayer. Record memory verses learned and review frequently.

Family Sabbath Activities

1. Examine your Seventh-day Adventist Christian roots. Make a family tree that begins with the first Adventist in your family.

2. Taking turns, recite as many memory verses as you can remember. See if you can increase the total next week.

3. Someone chooses a Bible character, animal, object, or location from the Bible and others ask "yes" or "no" questions. The one who names the object then thinks of the next subject to be guessed.

4. Using a designated version of the Bible, one person begins reading any somewhat familiar chapter. As she/he slowly continues reading, others search their Bibles to locate the passage.

Successful locators begin reading along until all the family members are reading in unison.

5. Assign characters of a Bible story to those present. Then dramatize the roles of each character and tape record it.
6. Research history and events based on the children's Sabbath School to enrich the week's study.
7. Dad or Mom can tell a story with a spiritual application from their childhood—ideally around a campfire in some special nature spot.
8. Older children can read Christian storybooks to younger siblings.

Adolescents and teenagers will be ready to take on deeper subjects of spiritual study:

1. As our sons grew older, we discovered that they actually enjoyed studying the book of Revelation and end-time events. At times their friends joined us around our oval dining room table.
2. Announce to your family, as if the event actually were a front page story, the following headline: "ALL TO WORSHIP ON SUNDAY; VIOLATIONS SUBJECT TO FULL PENALTY OF THE LAW." Ask the family for their individual responses. *Discuss:* after reading this, how important does Sabbath keeping seem now?
3. On the subject of the Sabbath, find Bible texts or Ellen White quotes. Ask the family to think of a "one-liner" summary that fits the section. These can be recorded in a Family's Spiritual Journey notebook.
4. *Dialogue:* "Our (my) destiny is in our (my)

hands." What does this mean? Can we say "our" destiny as a family?

5. Study the following passages that address the Sabbath topic and then endeavor to share the good news with someone who is not a Sabbath keeper:

From the Bible:

Genesis 2:2-3	Ezekiel 20:20
Leviticus 23:32	Ezekiel 20:12
Psalm 95:6	Matthew 12:12
Psalm 113:3	Revelation 14:12
Psalm 122:1	Exodus 20:20
Isaiah 55:6, 7	Revelation 22:14
Isaiah 58:13-14	Revelation 3:7-8

From Ellen White:

Child Guidance, pp. 53, 528, 530, 536-537.

Testimonies, vol. 1, pp. 532-537.

Patriarchs and Prophets, pp. 296, 307-308.

More references may be found by using the Ellen White Index or by searching on the Legacy of Light CD, available at your Adventist Book Center or from the Ellen G. White Estate at the General Conference of Seventh-day Adventists.

Researching the Sabbath is an exceptionally excellent study for teens and young married couples who may be experiencing a stage of reevaluating their values and Christian beliefs. How wonderful if this questioning is settled before the young people become parents.

More Spiritual Activities

1. Set up a flannel board, and as Mother or Father

reads, the child puts up the corresponding flannel items. Children may take turns. Let children retell the story themselves, using the picture they have created.

2. Each Sabbath study a different Seventh-day Adventist doctrine and review familiar ones.
3. Complete an entire Voice of Prophecy course as a family.
4. From the Acts account, determine the locations Paul worked and record them on a map. Sketch an icon representing what happened at each place.
5. Attend an Orthodox Jewish synagogue on Friday evening and observe how the present-day Jews keep the Sabbath.
6. Play the Bible Sword Drill game. Call out a book of the Bible and see who can find it. The first to locate it will announce the next book to be found.
7. Invite another family over to play a Bible game.
8. Stimulate the family's "sanctified imagination" by discussing the following:
   - What activities are going on in heaven this Sabbath?
   - What will the celebration in heaven be like when the redeemed come home?
   - Do you have some requests you would like to send up in advance for your mansion?
   - Try to imagine your angel's name. Until you find out, would you like to give your angel a name?

9. Make a Sabbath Book of Memories for the family.
10. On a cold winter night or long summer day, have everyone find a spiritual story to read or tell the family Sabbath afternoon.
11. Invite each one to read her/his favorite poem, if they have one.
12. Preview next week's Sabbath School lesson during the Sabbath rest time.
13. Rewrite a Bible story, adding the probable feelings of each character.

Activities for Tiny Tots

Little children have so short an interest span that it is challenging to know how to keep the Sabbath hours joyful. A number of young children intensifies the challenge. Selfish desires are put on the back burner in favor of family needs. The little ones need a lot of priority time. When I visited the Haloviak home when Kendra was a toddler, I was impressed how important educational activities were to them—telling her stories and playing Sabbath games—when I knew they were tired and would have preferred a little nap.

A parent relates how her daughter with three children under the age of five was approached in church by an older Christian lady: "These are the best years of your life!"

"If these are the best years of my life, why do I keep crying?" responded the young mother.

How nice if some mature church mothers would volunteer their help by telling stories and watching the little ones for a while on Sabbath afternoon so Mom and Dad could have a short time for undisturbed devotional reading or a little nap. Wishful thinking, perhaps, but if you have a real need, young parents, pray that God will send someone to help you. Caring for little ones corresponds to a twenty-four-hour nursing job.

Here are a few ideas that may be of help to young parents in endearing the Sabbath to their little ones:

1. Make a Sabbath felt board or box with felt animals, people, and items to focus a child's interest on Bible and nature topics.
2. Teach the children that Sabbath, the "Happy Day," is different from the rest of the week by keeping a special basket of Sabbath toys just for Sabbath hours.
3. Use finger plays with hand motions that teach them of God's goodness. Find these finger play books at your Adventist Christian Book Center.
4. Provide Sabbath coloring books with cut-outs and paste-on pictures.
5. Play or sing Cradle Roll and Kindergarten songs.
6. Do the Sabbath School lesson activities from the parents' quarterlies for Cradle Roll and Kindergarten.
7. Read to, converse with, and pray for, the little ones even though they don't seem to understand. Bonding takes place.
8. Read from A Child's Steps to Jesus or the Ladder of Life series to small children. Stories deal with themes such as kindness, unselfishness, helpfulness, and acceptance.

Never Give Up!

Satan desires our children, but we cannot give them up. At the altar of prayer we must keep fighting for them. As Winston Churchill said in his famous speech, "Never give up! Never give up! Never give up!"

How patient and prayerful parents must be in leading their children to love the Sabbath as God's gift. Remember that the Holy Spirit can teach the younger generation—and all of us—more in a moment about the joy of Sabbath keeping than we ever can.

Family Activity

Recall some of the times that Sabbaths were a delight to you.

CHAPTER NINE

What better time to affirm academy students than on Sabbath eve? Just a simple message will do: "I am so thankful that you are a part of our family, and Mom and I just want to say we miss you and love you."

PLANNING FOR "UNIQUE" SABBATHS

Often when traveling our Sabbaths are unique and need to be approached in a creative manner. Esther Knott tells that when they travel and stay in a hotel over the Sabbath they like to leave a note for the purpose of lightening the burden of the maid who cleans the room.

They write:

Dear Housekeeper:

We invite you to take a break. You need not clean or make up our room today. As Seventh-day Adventist Christians, we believe God's word in the Bible clearly calls us to a blessing of rest from normal work on the Sabbath day—

Saturday. He asks us to extend that blessing to others. We are delighted to extend it to you.

God bless you and Happy Sabbath!

Ron, Esther, and Olivia
Room 111

And they always leave a tip. Just think if all Adventists at a convention did that what a message it would be. People would get a blessing because we extended the Sabbath to them.

The Bad-Weather Sabbath

The wind is blowing, it's snowing, or the rain is pouring. What do parents do?

Now if we knew a bad snowstorm was predicted, we would go the Adventist Book Center and obtain a new, exciting storybook to read during the housebound Sabbath hours. We would begin the book Friday evening at sundown, and take turns reading throughout the Sabbath. Someone would read while Mom was preparing a meal, and while someone would be rinsing the dishes, someone else would be reading.

One Sabbath, I recall, it had taken us three days to shovel our driveway. On Sabbath morning there still was no movement on the road. The adventurous Wes and his father used cross-country skis to get to church! The rest of the few present walked and the pastor came by in a snowmobile. Mom decided to stay home and study the Bible. The fireplace was an important part of that snow-storm Sabbath.

It is the kind of day when the family can all snuggle under a warm, big blanket and listen to Mom and Dad tell stories about when they were children. When Dad would tell stories of himself as a boy missionary, our boys would project themselves in a foreign land one day and make believe the experiences they would have as real live missionaries. What fun!

Another "feature time" on a housebound Sabbath is to draw the stories being heard as someone reads or as the Your Story Hour tape plays (see example of Mark 16:1–8). Drawing the full story in sequence will occupy quite a segment of time on a bad weather day. When the sequence is complete, allow time for the drawer to retell the scenes. The story will be wonderfully remembered. Remember: that which you give mentally you keep—mentally.

Compile the family drawings and create a *Family Illustrated Bible.*

Some families meet the bad-weather challenge straight on. Why not make memories with the whole family toting umbrellas, walking in the rain? Or, if it is snowing giant flakes, bundle the family in many

WHO WILL ROLL THE STONE AWAY FOR US?
VERSE 3
VERSE 4
DO NOT BE ALARMED. YOU ARE LOOKING FOR JESUS WHO WAS CRUCIFIED. HE HAS RISEN! HE IS NOT HERE.
GO TELL HIS DISCIPLES, 'HE IS GOING AHEAD OF YOU INTO GALILEE, THERE YOU WILL SEE HIM.'
VERSES 5-7
VERSE 8

layers and take an invigorating walk together that will produce rosy cheeks? You may find that this is "what memories are made of."

Many of the suggestions in the previous chapter on Sabbath activities may be adapted to bad-weather Sabbaths.

Sabbath Miles Apart

The value of AT&T and MCI stock must go up on Friday night. It is the "homesick night" for Mom and Dad and their children at boarding school or college, or for their adult children who live at a distance, perhaps with children of their own.

On that night, we have time to communicate the language of love to those who are dear and special to us. We visit, share the weekly answers to prayer, and prayer victories.

At our house, Grandpa frequently emails the grandchildren a special story. If the story is a continued story, especially, the children may run excitedly to the screen. After the stories, Grandpa John reminds the children that their swing at our house is waiting for them.

Academy students also need love messages, and what better time to affirm them than on Sabbath Eve: "I am so thankful that you are a part of our family, and Mom and I just want to say that we miss you and love you."

Some children are separated from one parent because of a divorce. These electronic connections can help, especially, to fill the hole in their soul on the weekends that they miss, and are not visiting, their absent parent.

What better time to draw your family together and affirm them, even if it be electronically in the chat room or just on email, than Sabbath Eve.

Chapter Ten

I believe the Sabbath hours provide an excellent time for sharing love in all five love languages.

Creative Strategies for Sabbath Worships

The phone rang late one Friday evening. An excited parent related, "I just had a most joyful and satisfying experience. The moment was just right. The Holy Spirit was ministering to Brent and I could feel his heart being touched, so I led him to accept Jesus as his Savior for the first time! Then we prayed, as Brent repeated after me:

'I choose You, Jesus, and want You in my heart.
Please help me to want to be the kind of person
I should be.
I have sinned in so many ways.
Forgive me of my sins and clean me of them.

Take back any ground I have given Satan
by my actions.
I love You very much, and want to be in Your
heavenly kingdom.
In the name of Jesus I pray. Amen.'"

What a beautiful thing to do on Friday night—when the family is in a relaxed, pensive mood! You, too, can create such a moment, and then extend it by sharing with your child, in turn, how you accepted Jesus. Include details as to what happened, where, and how you felt during that special moment.

Another Friday evening "success story"

Martha, a young adult, had grown up in a Christian home. Every Friday evening the family had a delicious, traditional meal, followed by a special worship with sharing time. Then she found herself far from home at a new job with new friends. There was a pulling away from home values. One day she decided that Mother and Dad's religion was no longer for her and she determined to do her own thing.

But at home, there had been something special about Friday evening, and on Friday evening her thoughts kept returning home. She recalled the special Friday evening meals with the yummy cinnamon rolls, holding worship in the comfortable family room, and how the place was quiet but for the crackling fire in the fireplace. Sometimes they had laughed; sometimes they had cried.

Now on Friday night she was all alone. No special food. No sparkling clean house. No clean bed, nor freshly washed clothes. Besides, she missed Dad and Mom.

The Holy Spirit was impressing her with nostalgic thoughts. She began to think that she also was missing the God of her parents. Besides, she needed Jesus back in her life. Things were not going right without Him.

One Friday evening, alone in her small apartment across the country from home, she wondered what Mom and Dad were doing. She was sure they were having family worship together, and praying—most likely praying for her.

That night Martha's heart was softened as she listened to the gentle voice of the Holy Spirit. In tears, Martha made her way to the phone. Far away, this is what her parents heard: "Mom, Dad, I love you; I want you to know that I have decided to give my heart back to Jesus and ask Him to forgive me."

Even toddlers, too young to know about accepting Jesus, can find great pleasure in being told stories about Him. In turn, parents rejoice when hearing their little one repeat the name of Jesus the first time when pointing to His picture in a small book and asking, "Who is that?"

The parents' next step is, "Jesus loves Mommy and Daddy, and we love Jesus. Do you love Jesus?" The child responds "Yes!" and it was worships like these that became so much a part of the lives of Brent and Martha that how could they be anything but homesick on Friday night?

How Do We Do It?

How do we arrange so special a setting? The Sabbath is a bonding day. Father is finally home with time for his family. The love cup needs to be filled to overflowing again. The Sabbath hours provide time for hugs and kisses (especially for grandparents who may be "skin hungry"), love talks, and acts of appreciation. The Jewish people used these moments to affirm one another. In our home, Grandma received her affirmation after worship when she was tucked into bed for the evening. We told her she was getting her *succie,* which means "kiss" in Norwegian.

In Gary Chapman's book, *The Five Love Languages of Children,* he explains that we each receive and offer love in different love languages. Inherent in each person is a primary love language.

Chapman's five ways of saying "I love you" are physical touch, words of affirmation, quality time, gifts, and acts of service. My primary love language is acts of service. People can tell me every day that they love and appreciate me, but if they never help me with difficult tasks, I don't feel very loved.

When Jenny, our granddaughter, overheard us discussing love languages, I asked her, "Which of these makes you feel special?"

After a time of some pensive thought, Jenny finally said, "I feel loved when people do things with me." Jenny's love language is quality time with others.

I have a feeling that when parents don't feel their children really love them, and vice-versa, someone is not communicating in the right love language. It seems that as a mom, my primary love language when the boys were home was feeding the family good food. I later discovered that I had been speaking the wrong love language during those years. I have since endeavored to identify the primary love language of each family member.

One of the touching love languages our grandchildren greatly enjoy is getting a foot massage on Friday evening as we lounge around with the sacred music playing. This is not only calming, but it speaks of love. And it's free! Their father likes someone to give him a back message especially when he has done some hard construction work.

I believe the Sabbath hours provide an excellent time for sharing love in all five love languages. Gary Chapman highly recommends these five languages of love for every family. Think of it this way—on Sabbath we are bilingual! And when we speak the right love language, there are rewards.

How can we commence the Sabbath by starting out in the right love languages?

Through the years we often have noted the special touches that make the Sabbath worship experiences unique, from our own home, and others. May we share some with you?

As the worship hour approaches, our first matter for attention is the counsel of James 5:16: "Let all bitterness and wrath and malice be expelled from the soul. In a humble spirit, confess your faults one to another, and pray one for another, that ye may be healed." This can be done across the miles when there is a break in the relationship of family members. When someone says, "Forgive me" it feels so good and with it comes healing.

Yes, the Sabbath is for healing. To bask in a guilt-free Sabbath, with no silent treatment, ugly words, or thorns, we try to make things right. I recall once when, during one of those last minute pushes before sundown, I made some critical comment to son Wes in an unbecoming way.

Realizing my mistake, I bounded downstairs as Wes was skipping upstairs. As we passed, I darted an apology: "Wes, sorry I got so uptight!"

From the top of the stairs by then, he called back, "Oh, that's all right Mom; I made you get mad!" Even though we smile now at this on-the-run apology, it did clear the air. The simple words, "I'm sorry" carry a paralanguage of healing and peace. Like God, Satan has gifts for the Sabbath: anger, resentment, hostilities. These gifts Satan uses to torpedo a beautiful Sabbath experience. Don't let him!

The next preparation for the onset of Sabbath was to start a console recording that could be heard nicely throughout the house. Our traditional hymn was "How Long Has It Been Since You Talked to the Lord?" as the family crawled into their freshly made up beds on Friday evening.

When Esther Knott's parents desired her to realize that the Sabbath was special, they gave her a Sabbath nightie that was saved for only Friday evening. Esther always was excited about getting to wear her nightie on Friday night for worship, and she has passed on the tradition to her little daughter, Olivia, to make sweet memories of the Sabbath hours.

Now the family is ready to light the Sabbath candles and sing "Day Is Dying in the West," or one of the Jewish Sabbath songs. In the summer, the Sabbath Eve meal best precedes worship, and in the winter, worship can be integrated into the meal. Now, let the Sabbath worship begin!

Suggestions for Sabbath Worships

1. To avoid interruptions, cut the telephone off before worship.
2. Write a letter to God individually, or as a family, and share.
3. Pantomine Bible stories, such as those of Joseph, Moses, Elisha, or Paul. The family may guess the story and where it is found.
4. Children may draw a story in sequence that is read to them. When completed, the child may

use the illustrations to retell the story.

5. From Proverbs, create two lists of the wise and the foolish.
6. Sing the same Sabbath songs each Friday evening, such as "Day Is Dying in the West," or one of the Jewish songs.
7. Let it become a family tradition to memorize and repeat the fourth commandment, Psalm 91, or other meaningful texts.
8. Ask each person to pray, beginning with the youngest.
9. Pray in a special way for grandparents.
10. Hug everyone in the family at the close of worship and on Friday evening wish them Happy Sabbath. "Feliz Sábado" in Spanish. On Sabbath evening wish them a happy, blessed week.
11. Choose a favorite, former devotional book for guests. Ask the date of their birthdays (not necessarily the year), and then read the corresponding devotion for that day. It is fun to record the person's name on that page, and the place it was read. The devotional book then becomes a birthday book containing fond memories.
12. Begin an intercessory prayer list with four names to pray for each Sabbath Eve. Each time a prayer is answered, add another name. Record the answer in a Sabbath "Miracle Book."
13. During worship on Friday morning, read a selection on Sabbath preparation (such as "The Observance of the Sabbath" in *Testimonies,* vol. 6) and announce the times of sunset and sunset worship.

14. On Sabbath morning, read a selection on how to keep the Sabbath holy.

15. Record your family's goals for the Sabbath in a Family Worship Book. Add to it frequently, and occasionally reread for Sabbath worships.

16. Write appreciation notes to family members once a month.

17. Light two Sabbath candles on Friday night, one for Creation and one for Redemption. Re-light the candles on Sabbath evening to extinguish at the close of Sabbath.

18. Read an exciting mission story.

19. Play a Bible game from the Adventist Book Center.

20. Hold worship in an elderly church member's home.

In the summer, when sunset is delayed until nearly bedtime, the family may venture out into nature for Friday evening worship. How distinctly we remember the boys catching fireflies at Pathfinder Hill and then walking home through the woods in the darkness without a flashlight. In familiar woods, walk in the dark. Just in case—take along a flashlight.

Sometimes we built a campfire at Warren Dunes, and Dad told the boys stories of his life. Once we sat on the cliff wall overlooking the Atlantic Ocean and sang all the songs we knew about water and oceans. At our mountain cabin, we like to go to a favorite curve and sing "Like the Woman at the Well."

Chapter Eleven

"Singing . . . is as much an act of worship as is prayer."

(Patriarchs and Prophets, p. 594)

Sabbath Music

Music has the unique ability to "set the mood," both before and during an occasion. For me, sacred music can induce a lively and joyful atmosphere for Sabbath, and I am saddened when some of our denominational college radio stations play sad requiems during Sabbath hours.

Although the music we choose for our home is conservative, it is indeed happy. Surprisingly, many of the traditional Jewish songs are written in a minor key. Yet they are sung rapidly, and stimulate joyous feelings. Some are shared in this chapter.

Occasionally, when I am traveling alone and my heart is full of joy, the angels and I have a wonderful time together creating praise songs. I have surprised myself with the words and the melody that comes floating heavenward with a joyful heart.

In our community, we discovered that Kathryn Myers, better known locally as "Kay Bee," writes songs. "Come to Worship" is a song she wrote for calling the family together for worship. When we wanted a new worship song for the Friday welcome and the Sabbath closing, we asked Kay Bee. She wrote for us, "Welcome, Welcome Sabbath Day." This joyful song, with exceptionally meaningful words for Sabbath keepers, is also in a minor key and resembles Jewish Sabbath music. We think that the melody is delightful. We hope you enjoy including this special work in your Friday and Sabbath evening worship times.

Music is a major component of family time, for it touches the heart of each one of us, and often becomes a prayer to the Father. Accordingly, we take great care in our home in selecting the type of music played in our worship experience, and in our home at any time.

At the sunset hour we traditionally sing, "Day Is Dying in the West." Now we sing "Welcome, Welcome Sabbath Day" but only the first stanza. Families with small children might choose, "Sabbath Is a Happy Day." Sabbath morning the Youngberg's family musical alarm clock was a rousing rendition of "The King Is Coming!"

We trust that the following activities will heighten your family's enjoyment of sacred music during the Sabbath span from sunset to sunset:

Music Activities

1. Hum a song and have the family guess its title.
2. Sing selections from the *Christ in Song* hymnal.

3. Learn some Christian songs in the language of forefathers.
4. Memorize one new song each Sabbath, and continue to practice old ones from memory.
5. Play a special tape each Friday evening to introduce worship, such as "How Long Has It Been?" and another favorite as the family beds down. An exhilarating one to rise by on Sabbath morning is "The King Is Coming."
6. Play soft music during meal times.
7. Buy a new tape or CD once a month and save it for Sabbath to play the first time.
8. Sing the Word. Find as many songs as you can that are Words of Scripture.
9. Assemble family and friends for a sing-fest around the piano, or to play musical instruments.
10. Begin a prelude of relaxation before Sabbath by starting soft music an hour before sundown.
11. Musical families might compose a song based on their own favorite Sabbath theme or Scripture promise. These could be combined into one "family production."

Music Section

Come to Worship

As we read and pray to - geth - er; As we sing our wor - ship song;
In both sun-shine and storm-y weath-er, God will keep our fam - 'ly strong.

Welcome, Welcome Sabbath Day

(Part 1)

WELCOME, WELCOME SABBATH DAY
(PART 2)

Hevenu Shalom Aleicheim

Eliahu, Hanavi

Eliahu, Hanavi
Eliahu, hanavi
Eliahu, hatishbi
Eliahu, hagiladi.
Bimhera iavo eleinu
Im mashi'ach ben David

Translation:

Elijah the Prophet
Elijah, the prophet
Elijah, of Teshve
Elijah, of Gil'ad,
Will come to us soon,
With the Messiah, son of David

אֱלִיָּהוּ הַנָּבִיא
עממי

אֱלִיָּהוּ הַנָּבִיא,
אֱלִיָּהוּ הַתִּשְׁבִּי,
אֱלִיָּהוּ הַגִּלְעָדִי —
בִּמְהֵרָה יָבוֹא אֵלֵינוּ
עִם מָשִׁיחַ בֶּן דָּוִד.

SABBATH BLESSING

Public domain.

Shabbat Hamalkah/ Queen Sabbath

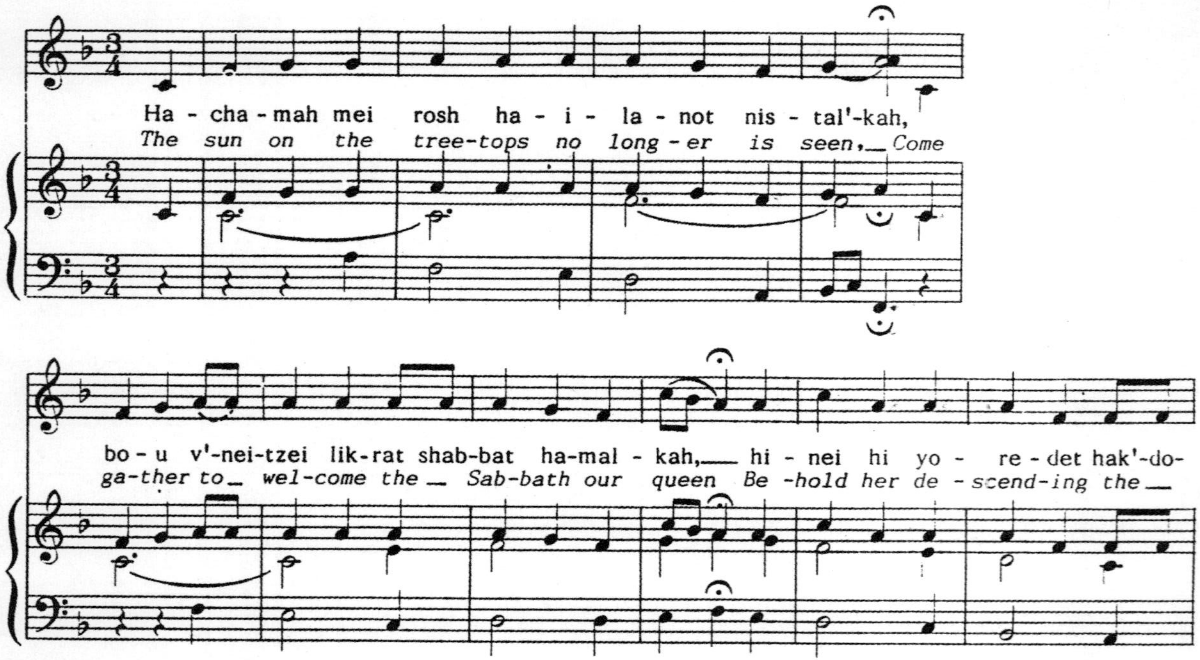

From Gates of Song: Music for Sabbath. *P. Minkowsky arr. H. Fromm*
Hebrew text: Ch. N. Bialik, English text: A. I. Cohon, Transcontinental Music Publications, New Jewish Music Press, 838 Fifth Ave., New York, NY 10021-7064. ISBN 88074-0407-1. Tel. 212-650-4121, FAX 212-650-4119. #158.

Bo - i, bo - i, ha - mal - kah! Bo - i, bo - i,
near, draw near, and here a - bide, Draw near, draw near, O
ha - ka - lah! Sha - lom a - lei - chem mal-a - chei ha - sha - lom.
Sab - bath bride. Peace al - so to you, you an - gels of peace.

Chapter Twelve

"The Sabbath is a golden clasp that unites God and His people."

(Testimonies, 6:351)

Close of the Sabbath

Our Jewish friends begrudgingly say good-bye to the Sabbath each week. In fact, they don't consider the Sabbath to be over until they can see five stars (in good weather, we presume).

How do we feel when the Sabbath closes? Relieved? Ecstatic? Regretful? Do we truly believe the quotation (on the left side of this page) that during the Sabbath hours the families of earth and heaven are specially united?

A few moments before the sun sets on Friday evening, families often form a circle to sing a song, pray, and wish one another a happy week. Our family joins the Spanish in saying, Feliz Sábado, which means "Happy Sabbath!" For Sabbath evening we say, Feliz Semana, which means "Happy Week!"

If you want to bid farewell to the Sabbath with a Jewish flavor, we would suggest you sing the last stanza of Kathryn Myers's song "Welcome, Welcome, Sabbath Day." As their lighting of the Sabbath candles signaled the beginning of the Sabbath, the extinguishing of candles signals it's close. In many homes the children are allowed, under supervision, to relight the Sabbath candles about twenty minutes before sundown, and a child is delegated to blow them out at the close of Sabbath.

This would be a sad moment, but for their special transition from the Sabbath candles to a special Sabbath fragrance intended to linger with them through the week. This lingering fragrance will carry them ahead until the Sabbath candles can be lit once again.

Accordingly, a little ceremony is designed to extinguish the Sabbath candles and distribute among the family a little spice box, called basseman. Basseman represents the fragrance of life that has just been experienced during the Sabbath. The essence of this little Sabbath-closing ceremony is captured in the following family litany I (John) wrote. This litany should serve to stimulate thought among the participants as the family moves through the process.

The two Sabbath candles are re-lit before the litany, and designations conferred as to who will extinguish them at the appropriate time and who will light the incense. Children love this involvement. Twisted candles are effective in symbolizing the togetherness the family has just enjoyed in the Sabbath experience. Twisted candles may also represent how Creation and Redemption are linked together.

The litany is designed for a family of four: A: father, B: mother, C: and D: children. Parts may be doubled according to the number available. For the public meeting, the parts may be adapted: A: minister or leader, B: men (or one side of the room), C: women (or one side of the room), D: children. *Other variations are possible.*

Unless participants **B, C,** and **D** are creatively spontaneous, allow them time beforehand to contemplate their responses to their open-ended lines. All involved should be familiar with, and thoroughly understand, the significance of their parts.

Family Sabbath Celebration Covenant

A litany to close the Sabbath

A: Oh, day of rest and gladness,
You are a day of love.

B: A day to raise affection
From earth to things above.

C: We have learned from God's Word:
_______________ (name one thing).

D: We have learned from God's Word:
_______________ (name one thing).

E: We have sought to do good to others:
_______________ (name one thing).

A: In this earth we have no continuing city
No place that will endure.

C: Thank You, God, for sharing with us
This palace in time.

ALL: Which will abide through all eternity.

B: There are three reasons why we love You.
Yes, there are four reasons we adore You on the Sabbath day.

D: We praise You for Creation,
We honor you for dying on the cross,
and resting.

C: We trust You to bring victory in the final test,
And we long for the Sabbath rest You have
promised in the New Earth.

A: Oh Sabbath, as champions forsake You,
As standard-bearers trample your colors in
the dust,

ALL: We will arise to defend God's down-trodden
law.

B: Lord, make us "repairers of the breach."

ALL: And "restorers of paths to dwell in."

A: And now, as the sun has sunk into the West,

B: And as the candle goes out into darkness
*[lights the incense, then blows out the
Sabbath candles]*
Our hearts mourn the passing of your
pleasant hours.

A: We are sad to see the Queen leave us.

B: We take up again the tasks of another week,
Asking that the sweet incense of Your presence
Remain with us in our labor and play,
Until six days hence.

ALL: We rejoice again in the "golden clasp" that
joins God and His people.

Litany or not, the burning of a candle at the dimming of the Sabbath day has a quieting effect on the family during these special moments of closing worship. The family recognizes that the new week does not begin until the candle is extinguished, signaling that the Sabbath has ended.

One last impression that helps ease the family into this transition that the Sabbath indeed has slid into a new week is to take the family together outside to watch in the heavens for the first five stars of the night. The family returns inside refreshed by the invigorating evening air and eager to begin the activities of a new week—perhaps to make a batch of popcorn to contribute to the fireside munchies.

Closing Sabbath for Teens

When our sons were teenagers, we guarded these final moments of Sabbath by cutting the telephones during closing worship. Teenagers, who want to be with their friends, may become "antsy" as sundown approaches. Invariably we would be in the middle of prayer when one of their friends would call just to find out what the boys were going to do that evening.

Suggestion: if their friends are invited over for sundown worship, these problems may not arise.

In another home, as a guest myself during the closing moments of Sabbath, I came upon another suggestion for keeping teenagers actively interested in these closing moments. After prayer, the girls were about to run out of the house for a Saturday night activity with their friends when one exclaimed, "We haven't written in the Sabbath memory book yet!"

My curiosity was piqued: What is a Sabbath Memory book? After the girls had located and entered a few thoughts in the well-used book, they were on their way. Now I could query their parents to fill me in on the background of this important phenomenon.

It seems the family had weathered some difficult,

discouraging times, when they had dwelt more on the negatives in life than the positives. That was when they decided to take time to start recording the positive blessings on their lives each Sabbath. This recording process became a tradition. Later, when discouraging events would surface, they would read the Sabbath Memory Book, and recall these recorded rich blessings.

I call this, "I spy God in my life."

Do you spy God blessing your Sabbath celebrations?

Chapter Thirteen

"At this time we must gather warmth from the coldness of others, courage from their cowardice, and loyalty from their treason."

(Testimonies, 5:136)

Sabbath-Keeping Families in the Last Days

When the Children of Israel came out of Egypt, God gave them the Ten Commandments. The fourth became their visible identifying mark that they were God's chosen people to the nations around, as they saw them observing the Sabbath.

In the last days on earth, the focus of Sabbath keeping once again will be the identifying mark of God's chosen people as the world will see them observing the Sabbath. At that time, the Sabbath will advance from being an identifying mark to an identifying test.

As we approach that time, an important, all-consuming question arises for meditation:

If we cannot pass the small tests in regard to Sabbath keeping now (when we allow our work to overlap its hours, or when we enjoy pleasures on the Sabbath that distance us from Christ, rather than drawing us nearer to Him), will the Sabbath—at some future time—all at once mean so much to us that we are willing to lay down our lives for it to prove our loyalty?

The loyalty is, of course, to God. The Sabbath is but a test of that loyalty.

The fourth commandment is not just a suggestion. It is a requirement and the subject of the whole battle of evil and good between the two kingdoms. The battle is a critical test of allegiance to the King of kings.

During the communist regime in Czechoslovakia believers in the Sabbath were watched and sometimes falsely portrayed as anti-government as they influenced workers not to labor on the Sabbath. Under these dangerous circumstances the faithful would gather in the home of one of the believers and spend all night and the daytime hours of the Sabbath together in muffled worship with the curtains drawn. Usually they would come in one or two at a time to avoid suspicion and after the Sabbath had passed leave in the same way.

However, spies were watching and one Friday night a raid was made by the police. That particular Friday evening some of the believers were ill and did not come to worship on Friday evening. "What is going on here?" the police demanded.

But that night the only ones who had arrived were all relatives. "These are our family members. They have come to visit with us," was the honest reply. Again God through unusual circumstances had spared His children who were keeping His Sabbath holy.

Our neighbor, Stanley Maxwell, tells the story of Mr. Wong in his exciting book, *The Man who Couldn't Be Killed.* Imprisoned during China's Cultural Revolution and sentenced to hard labor during years of "reeducation," he continued to keep every Sabbath holy. Commanded to work, he was mobbed for disobedience, pushed down, kicked, hit, and pounded upon. For hours the process continued. Guards fingered the triggers on their weapons as they demanded that he join the work detail. Mr. Wong pitied the pain-givers and prayed for their forgiveness. For six months the beatings continued every Sabbath and then abruptly stopped and he was permitted to worship his Real God as he saw best. Originally 1,500 prisoners had been sent from Shanghai to the camp in Thinghai Province. Over the 20 years of his imprisonment 3,500 more were sent to join them. After two decades only 18 of the 5,000 were left and Mr. Wong was one of five who were released.

We can't really finish this chapter on earth. It will be finished in heaven when the persecutions of the last fearful time of trouble will all be passed and when we will have already proved our loyalty to the fourth commandment under a death decree, and gained the victory by the blood of the Lamb.

But until then . . .

When the laws of many nations and the courts brand Sabbath keepers as enemies of society, what will we do? Will we tread on God's holy day and revere another day in its place? What will we do when former teachers among us turn against us and pronounce us legalists and stubborn? When our friends abandon the Sabbath, will we stand firm?

"As champions forsake the ranks, and standard-bearers permit the colors to trail in the dust; when defenders of the faith are few, then strong courageous hearts must come to the front. 'At this time we must gather warmth from the coldness of others, courage from their cowardice, and loyalty from their treason.'" (A statement by the General Conference Committee quoted in F.C. Gilbert, *Divine Predictions,* p. 296. The inner quote is from Ellen G. White, *Testimonies,* 5:136).

Here are some questions to consider regarding Sabbath celebration. Will we always be able to celebrate the Sabbath or because there is imminent persecution will the celebration be enhanced but in a quiet secluded place? Does the intense emotion of worshiping outside the protection of human law heighten a dynamic celebration or have you ever thought of this in respect to last-day persecution which prophecy points us to?

There are many who believe that the day is coming when Sabbath keepers will be proclaimed as law breakers, and as destroying society and causing God's judgments to fall on the world. The keepers of the true Sabbath will be accused of being the cause of horrific climatic changes which supposedly are taking place because of God's displeasure, because a group of obstinate fanatics will not worship on Sunday as the law requires. Under those circumstances will God's people celebrate the Sabbath? How? Think about it.

What about the celebration when families openly worship on the Sabbath knowing that the act will lead to persecution because they conscientiously refuse to keep the papal sabbath? Will they celebrate because they stood up for God's law and were faithful? Will the angels join them in the celebrations cheering on God's children?

The conflict is coming for sure when God's children will be put to the test as never before.

Chapter Fourteen

". . . no eye has seen, nor ear has heard, what the Lord has prepared for those who love Him."

Our First Celestial Sabbath

What a glorious celebration our first heavenly Sabbath will be "when all our labors and trials are o'er," and we will worship in the Holy City of God with Him who is the King of Glory, the Mighty God, the Everlasting Father and our Forever Friend.

All of the redeemed of the earth will worship in unity the victory of Christ Jesus who died for us and who proved to all the universes that God's law and day was vindicated and powerfully exalted.

As we think of that Sabbath Celebration day we realize that ". . . no eye has seen, nor ear has heard, what the Lord has prepared for those who love him." One thing for sure it will exceed the extravaganza of the worldwide celebration welcoming the new 2000 millennium. From all ages of time, from all nations of the world, the old and the young, the new believers and old ones will sing the song of Moses and the Lamb and praise the Victorious One with lofty alleluia in a mighty chorus, one octave and another and another in a mighty crescendo that will swell the heavens with praise.

Angels' harps and voices will join the redeemed in music beyond anything our ears have heard in the majestic, regal and most sublime Sabbath choir ever, ever, ever heard. What a Sabbath worship that will be! It will certainly be a celebration.

All will be energized as never before and the scenes with the city of gold and many colors and thousands and the thousands of joyful angels in the victorious atmosphere will fill the heavens with their flight of congratulation, flying from one to another of the redeemed. There will not be a sad tear there but perhaps happy tears of dynamic joy. The controversy is over and His heaven (at last!) was worth waiting and fighting for. The family of earth in their robes of righteousness and the family of God are one in the celestial Sabbath celebration.

And wherever that first celestial Sabbath will be celebrated doesn't really matter that much. Our greatest joy and unutterable thrill won't be palaces, acquaintances, visiting the Bible characters, or cosmic travel. My greatest joy will be to celebrate that first celestial Sabbath with Jesus. By God's grace let's all plan to be there with our families.

Family Activity: Celestial Sabbath Celebration

Record here how you imagine the first celestial Sabbath celebration:

Chapter Fifteen

". . . turn away from trampling on the Sabbath, from doing your pleasure on My holy day, but rather call the Sabbath a delight, the holy day of the Lord honorable, and you honor Him . . ."

(Isaiah 58:13)

Sabbath Activities for Families

Activity: Agree–Disagree

One family member reads the Agree–Disagree item. Then put thumbs up if you agree, thumbs down if you disagree. After all 7 items have been responded to with an agree or disagree, discuss as a family.

1. It would be helpful if the church would prepare a comprehensive list of what is lawful to do on the Sabbath and what is unlawful.
2. Most SDAs know why they keep the Sabbath but have difficulty in knowing how to keep the Sabbath.

3. Fathers can more easily keep the Sabbath than mothers.
4. If the Sabbath had always been kept, there would never have been an atheist or an infidel.
5. In the last days, Adventists will keep the Sabbath more faithfully than in years gone by.
6. Nine- and ten-year-old children should still be allowed to bring toys to church to keep them busy so they won't disturb others.
7. Sabbath keeping is more a matter of attitude than activity.

Activity: Sabbath Principles

Make a list of Sabbath observance principles.

Activity: Family Mission

As a family write a Family Mission Statement which includes a choice to keep the Sabbath day holy.

Family Activity: Weekly Preparation

Record duties and activities that need to be accomplished each week in the home so that it will be kept clean and tidy and that will ensure readiness for the Sabbath.

Sunday

Monday

Tuesday

Wednesday

Thursday

Friday

Family Activity: Isaiah 58

Read these verses to remind the family what God promises when we celebrate His Sabbath.

Celebrating the Delights of Becoming Repairers of the Breach in the Family and in the Human Personality

"Is not this the kind of fasting I have chosen: to loose the chains of injustice and untie the cords of the yoke, to set the oppressed free and break every yoke? (verse 6).

"I want you to share your food with the hungry and bring right into your own homes those who are helpless, poor and destitute. Clothe those who are cold and don't hide from relatives who need your help (verse 7).

"Then your light will break forth like the dawn, and your healing will spring forth speedily, and your righteousness will be as a shield before you, and the glory of the Lord will be your rear guard (verse 8).

"Then you will call, and the Lord will answer; you will cry for help, and He will say, Here I am. If you take away the yoke of oppressing the weak, and stop making false accusations and spreading vicious rumors, (verse 9)

"if you spend yourself on behalf of the hungry and satisfy the needs of the oppressed, then your light will rise in the darkness, and your night will become like the noonday (verse 10).

"The Lord will guide you continually; He will satisfy your needs in a sun-scorched land, and will strengthen your bones; and you will be like a well-watered garden, like a spring whose waters never fail (verse 11).

"Those from among you will build the old waste places; you will raise up the foundations of many generations; and you will be called the Repairer of the Breach, and Restorer of paths in which to dwell (verse 12).

"If you turn away from trampling on the Sabbath, from doing your pleaseure on My holy day, but rather call the Sabbath a delight, the holy day of the Lord honorable, and you honor Him not doing your own ways, nor finding your own pleasure, nor speaking your own words, (verse 13)

"Then you will delight yourself in the Lord, and I will make you ride on the heights of the earth, and I will feed you with the heritage of Jacob your father. The mouth of the Lord has spoken" (verse 14).

Family Activity: Preparing for the Queen

1. If you were expecting royalty to spend a day with your family, how would you prepare?

   a.

   b.

   c.

   d.

   e.

2. When should the preparation for the Sabbath begin?

3. What criteria or principle could we use to distinguish if a given activity should be done as a preparation for the Sabbath or if it could properly be performed during the holy hours?

   a.

   b.

   c.

4. How can we prepare our spirits and not just our houses, premises and physical persons for the visit of the Queen?